LEADERSHIP UNDER FIRE

"When you walk through fire, you will not be burned."
Isaiah 43:2

LEADERSHIP UNDER FIRE

Developing Courageous Leaders for the Church

SCOTT WIGGINS
Brigadier General, USAF (Ret)

Leadership Under Fire: Developing Courageous Leaders for the Church

For information about this title or to order other books and/or electronic media, contact the publisher:

Scott Wiggins
http://www.scottwiggins.org
contact@scottwiggins.org

ISBNs:
979-8-9946298-0-2 (softcover)
979-8-9946298-1-9 (eBook)

Printed in the United States of America

Cover and Interior design: 1106 Design

Dedication

Thank you to Jennabeth Baker Wiggins.
You said "for better or worse" and live it everyday.

Thank you to Abby Wiggins Campbell
and Kate Wiggins Cheatham.
You bring light and life to the pages of my life.

★ ★ ★ ★ ★ ★ ★

Table of Contents

★★★★★★★

Foreword

I've been under fire. During my twenty-seven-year military career, the aggression had various origins. While flying combat sorties in Iraq, Afghanistan, and Somalia, small-arms fire was the principal threat. These enemy engagements were more annoying than threatening. Damage to the aircraft would affect mission readiness, but it was highly unlikely a bullet would cause severe or catastrophic results to the plane's airworthiness. It was even less likely a stray bullet would harm the pilot. Base attacks from our adversaries were more problematic. Rocket-propelled grenades (RPGs), mortars, vehicle-borne improvised explosive devices (VBIEDs), and suicide bombers were a few of the actions used against facilities where I was stationed. In many circumstances, the weapon was used with a "spray and pray" mentality, meaning targeting was minimal; the enemy was hoping their efforts would wound or kill. Many times, they were successful, but, just as many times, the weapon did little or no damage.

One surprising method of aggression came at Balad Air Base, Iraq. Some of the base support operations were provided by what we called "host-nation personnel." Iraqis would serve in certain functions. This is great for relations, but it can create some security risks for the citizens as well as the military. In one instance, an al-Qaeda supporter had a position working in the dining facility. Despite clearing security protocols, this individual was able to obtain a position and used their access to poison some of the food in the dining facility. Fortunately, the result was Disney World-type lines for the bathroom but no serious or permanent injuries. I can look back at the incident and laugh, but the possibility of a serious threat to personnel and the degraded ability to defend the base against an attack could have written a different story.

"Under fire," "taking fire," and "troops in contact" are all terms used to describe active engagement with an enemy. Following my time in the military, I transitioned to a position in ministry working at a local church. Unlike the battlefield, the ministry field had a different enemy with different tactics and weapons. The church's adversaries ranged from spiritual attacks by Satan to individuals and groups aligned against the church, even to internal assaults from other members of the staff or congregation. We live in a fallen world, so none of these actions surprised me. However, I was stunned by my observations that we were *aiding the enemy.* What was the treasonous activity? We nominate, endorse, employ, empower, and tolerate poor leadership. We allow our churches to be led and overseen by people who are unprepared and untrained, with disastrous results. My observations reminded me of a leadership conversation I'd had years earlier.

In June 2011, I was serving as the Commandant of the Air Force's Officer Training School (OTS). OTS is one of three commissioning sources for the Air Force, with the others being the United States Air Force Academy and the Reserve Officer Training Corps (ROTC). Each year, approximately three thousand men and women are commissioned as second lieutenants through OTS at Maxwell Air Force Base, Alabama. Then, a nine-week, four-phase program develops the trainees mentally, physically, and academically, preparing them to be officers in the United States Air Force.

OTS has a modified program called Commissioned Officer Training (COT). This course is tailored toward the National Guard and Air Force Reserves. The trainees are medical doctors, lawyers, pharmacists, and chaplains. Usually, they are practicing their trade as civilians; they are inspired to do their part, and they join the Reserves or Guard in their hometown. They receive an officer commission commensurate with their professional experience and attend the five-week training course.

After presiding over a COT class graduation, one of the students approached me. He introduced himself and made this comment: "Sir, I've been practicing medicine for eight years. I have my own practice, with another doctor, a couple of nurses, and an administrative staff. I think I'm a pretty good doctor. I found out over the last five weeks that I'm a terrible leader. Medical school provides no training in this area. I wish I had attended this course before I opened my own practice. While I'm still behind, I think I have a basic understanding as to what leadership is now. Thank you."

I was grateful for this Captain's honesty but shocked by the reality of what he was saying. Doctors, lawyers, chaplains, and others are leading businesses, staffs, and churches without any education, training, or experience in the art of leadership. They have technical skills but no understanding and, in many cases, no interest in learning how to steward the position they occupy.

Recalling this conversation and armed with my experience in the church, I had an epiphany. With rejuvenated motivation and discipline, I aspired to be a learner of and resource for the growth of leaders. A step in that process was to capture the stories of my journey along this path in hopes you will be inspired, convicted, and convinced of this worthy pursuit.

Leadership Under Fire: Developing Courageous Leaders for the Church examines how ineffective leadership has taken root in the church. It describes the qualities needed to guide our congregations and presents a plan to implement change. Bullets or RPGs were a threat to me and the people I served alongside in the military. Poor leadership is a strategic and tactical problem crippling the church. It's time to gird up, develop, and deploy courageous leaders.

★ ★ ★ ★ ★ ★ ★

Introduction

Our earliest opportunities to have a choice in leadership most likely were presented at school. Maybe the class decided who was going to be the line leader. Possibly there was an election regarding who would be captains during playground games. As we advanced, soon we were selecting class officers, student management of clubs or teams, as well as choosing royalty, like queens and kings of homecoming or the prom. What influenced our initial ballot decisions?

I imagine your school followed a similar path to the schools I attended in Conley Hills Elementary in East Point, Georgia, Myrtle Beach High School, Myrtle Beach, South Carolina, and Mountain Brook High School, in Mountain Brook, Alabama. Popularity, appearance, and excellence in performance, preferably in athletics, were the principal qualifiers.

Sadly, it appears we never progressed from these early influences. Maybe this rubric didn't adversely affect the leadership of the Parent Teacher Association (PTA), your local Rotary Club, Chamber of Commerce, or YMCA. I doubt that the world tumbled off of its axis because a football team, debate club, or local symphony was guided by someone skilled in sports, academics, or music. However, this method of selecting leaders has failed and is failing the local church.

Senior Pastors are selected based on their ability as spoken-word communicators. If someone has a gift in constructing a twenty-five-minute weekly message that entertains and has some measure of biblical foundation, the congregation turns the keys of leadership over to them. In turn, they lead other staff members, an oversight board, and a congregation of people, and the most important defining filter is that they tell a good story. Oversight, whether it is conducted by elders, deacons, or board members, is handed to people just as haphazardly. Qualifications range from people who are friends of the pastor, to important donors, and to individuals who just happen to have been at the church for decades. In this case, we've marginalized the qualification of "leader" to someone who is *liked, wealthy, or committed to attendance.* This is how we have attempted to carry out—and failed spectacularly—the direction of the Apostle Paul in the books of 1 Timothy and Titus regarding leadership qualification. Further, when we provide the same vetting and discernment for church leaders as we did when we divided up teams for a game of kickball at second-grade recess, we are failing in the mission that Jesus, who built the church, gave us.

These decisions have resulted in a failure of leadership. The church needs to take direct action to learn from and repair this negligence. Our first step is to confess our sin. Let's not sugarcoat this issue. We have sinned by not adhering to God's biblical direction and by adopting practices of the world that are contrary to His character. We need to understand the leadership qualities God desires for His church. Then, we need to train and equip people in those disciplines. Lastly, the church needs to continually review leadership's actions through the lens of God's definition.

This book is designed to lead you through this process. I will accomplish this by walking you through my growth and development as a Christian who had served professionally as a military officer. I'll describe the leadership lessons I learned and explain their context. Then, I'll tie this experience back to the Bible to ensure alignment with God's direction.

I served in combat operations in Desert Storm (Kuwait), Operation Support Hope (Rwanda), Operations Restore Hope and Gothic Serpent (Somalia), Operation Allied Force (Kosovo), Operation Iraqi Freedom and Operation Enduring Freedom (Afghanistan). The enemy of poor leadership in the church is just as evil and deadly as any warlord, extremist, terrorist, or dictator I faced. In fact, it's more deadly, because we've been willing participants. What is your answer to this question: do you favor the *religion of comfortableness*—as Friedrich Nietzsche called it—or do you stand on conviction even if you have to stand alone? It's time to accept our responsibility and lead in a manner that befits the one we call Savior and King. We surrendered the ground of leadership without firing a shot. It's time to take it back.

CHAPTER 1

★★★★★★★

Leadership: Is That the Right Word?

My wife, Jennabeth, is a voracious reader. This appetite has produced an impressive vocabulary. Whether it's spelling, proper definition, or accurate usage, she's a wordsmith (yes—that's a word). She'll frequently comment when she sees the King's English violated. She's helped me with my spelling through the years. Here's a test for you: is it "a lot" or "alot"; "bellweather" or "bellwether"; or "occasionaly" or "occasionally"? Is it proper phrasing to say "all of the sudden" or "all of a sudden"; "first-come, first-serve" or "first-come, first-served"; "I couldn't care less" or "I could care less"? And, what about correctly using a word such as "there" or "their" or using "travesty" (which means "false" or "distorted") when we mean "tragedy." What about using "peruse" (which means "to observe in depth") when we actually mean "skim" or "browse"?

Not only do we have a difficult time spelling accurately, speaking properly, and using words appropriately, but culture has its hand in the cookie jar when it comes to our lexicon. "Extra" can now be used to describe a person. My call sign in the military was "Wig," but a "wig" is also a head covering of real or artificial hair, and it currently also means "amazing." "Fit" means "of suitable quality or standard" but now adds the connotation of "attractive." "Fire" *does* mean "something that is combustible" but has the added meaning of "something that is cool or amazing." Forming a foundation is the definition of "basic" unless you're in chemistry class, when it means "having the properties of a base." If you're talking to a high-school student, "basic" describes someone or something that is very mainstream.

It's easy to see how landing on a working definition of anything is a challenge. The concept of *leadership* sits right in the middle of this quagmire of confusion. In the midst of this unclear definition, the industry that is leadership is booming. Amazon lists their top-ten non-fiction categories as biographies and memoirs; self-help; religion and spirituality; health, fitness and dieting; politics and social science; cookbooks; business and money; parenting and relationships; education and teaching; and crafts, hobbies, and home. Of these categories, six of the ten have forms of leadership books at the top of their charts. There are people who are an industry unto themselves in the area of leadership. Names like John Maxwell, Marshall Goldsmith, Ken Blanchard, Jim Collins, Simon Sinek, Robin Sharma, and Patrick Lencioni dot the landscape not only in print but also in consulting, motivational speaking, and leading conferences.

As a product of leadership training, I've read and listened to all of the top names and companies. Additionally, I've studied the finest United States Air Force institutions of leadership training and development. I was given a basic introduction to leadership at Officer Training School (OTS). In order to be commissioned as an officer in the Air Force, a candidate must successfully traverse through one of three commissioning sources—the United States Air Force Academy (USAFA), Reserve Officer Training Corps (ROTC), or the Officer Training School (OTS).

At OTS, the Air Force takes college graduates who are candidates to become officers through four phases of training. The first phase is military indoctrination, focusing on teamwork, standardization, discipline, and the fundamentals of leadership. Phase two focuses on the profession of arms and a growing understanding of leadership practice and management. Next, phase three adds the practical application of what the trainee has learned in the first two phases. These include leadership practicums involving specifically assigned areas of responsibility inside the trainee wing or flight as well as evaluation on the Leadership Reaction Course (LRC). The LRC is a series of challenges akin to an obstacle course, with added planning and intellectual challenges designed to test leadership traits, problem-solving under time constraints, and management of personnel and logistical resources. Phase four serves as a transitional period, moving from training to operational environments.

Following four years of service in the Air Force, I attended Squadron Officer School (SOS). Designed for captains, SOS exists to "develop solution-minded, bold, and courageous airmen ready to overcome today's and tomorrow's challenges." When you think of SOS, a reasonable parallel in the business world is "middle management." The three areas of design for the curriculum at SOS are leadership, strategic design, and multi-domain joint warfare.

Somewhere around year eight to year ten, an Air Force officer might be selected to attend Air Command and Staff College (ACSC). I completed this course in my ninth year. ACSC's purpose is to prepare you to lead at the squadron level. In the civilian sector, ACSC would prepare someone to lead a large department. A squadron can consist of anywhere between fifty and three-hundred people, depending on the unit's mission. This school helps you make the jump from leading ten to fifteen airmen to a larger contingency. Also, it adds skills necessary to work in air and space environments in a joint military campaign.

The last of the Air Force's professional military education (PME) officer courses is Air War College (AWC). The resident program lasts approximately a year, while the distance-learning version takes between nine and twelve months, depending on the student's existing military duties. I completed the distance-learning version with the added benefit of some weekend intensives I was invited to join. AWC is designed for the senior leaders of the military as well as specifically invited federal-government agencies.

AWC is on par with senior executive training. The desired learning outcomes from AWC are:

- lead successfully as senior leaders in joint, coalition, and interagency environments, exhibiting the traits essential to the profession of arms and understanding the proper role and employment of airpower capabilities
- critically analyze complex political-military issues and clearly articulate, through written and oral methods, solutions to influence senior-level decisions
- develop and shape military strategies, which, in concert with other instruments of national power, achieve national-security strategic objectives
- capitalize upon diverse personal and professional relationships forged from the broader AWC educational experience

I was very fortunate to complete every level of officer development as well as other leadership-training forums at the National Defense University and courses offered by the Air National Guard (ANG) and Air Force Reserves (AFRS). The United States and her taxpayers invested significant time and resources to train me to lead her sons and daughters as members of the Air Force. The information and education are world-class, but the greatest gift was taking that knowledge and putting it into practice.

I was a Flight Commander (58th Airlift Squadron, Altus Air Force Base, Oklahoma, leading fifteen men and women as well as the 183rd Airlift Squadron Mississippi Air National Guard, leading twelve), Squadron Commander (183rd Airlift Squadron, Mississippi Air National Guard, overseeing two-hundred), Group Commander (172nd Operations Group, leading three squadrons totaling five-hundred people), and Wing Commander (Officer Training School Commandant and Vice Commandant with a total instructor cadre and trainee population of more than three-thousand). This allowed me to exercise the theory of leadership with the practical execution of this knowledge for the purpose of accomplishing a mission to attain a vision.

While the military significantly shaped my understanding and definition of leadership, it wasn't the exclusive carrier of this quality.

My parents, Leo and Iris Wiggins, were principal instructors in my education.

Playing sports throughout my life was a great laboratory. I observed much and practiced some as a manager for the basketball team at the University of Alabama. While a public-relations assistant for the Atlanta Hawks, I observed highly successful men such as Ted Turner, Stan Kasten, and Bob Wolfe as they led organizations.

I had the best seat in the world watching my wife lead two daughters, who have become outstanding women. While it was a military assignment, the perspective on leadership I gained while serving with Air Force One for two years gave me an intriguing view of watching the President of the United States as well as other national leaders of politics and industry. I add the academic and practical training, mix it with observation, cook it under the pressure of leading organizations around the world, and I arrive at a unique perspective on leadership.

Before I advance a definition of leadership, I think it's important to recognize some disclaimers. First, I don't think the military knows everything about leadership. Some of the qualities of leadership that are invaluable in the military simply don't translate to civilian environments. Also, I don't think every person with military experience is a leader. Just because someone wore the uniform or went to the training doesn't mean they mastered the art. Also, I don't think you have to be talented in any given subject to have knowledge or wisdom of the subject. For example, Nick Saban didn't have a particularly noteworthy career as a college football player at Kent State University. Yet, you better make a space in Atlanta at the Chick-Fil-A College Football Hall of Fame as a coach, because he's arguably the best to have ever roamed the sidelines. Even though someone might not have led their cheerleading squad, wasn't the president of their fraternity, or wasn't the chairman of the chamber of commerce Christmas social doesn't mean they don't have the ability to speak into qualities surrounding leadership. My wife was never CEO of a Fortune 500 company, but I'll pick her over anyone in knowing how to develop and mentor a young woman.

The definition of leadership has been hijacked. It's been stolen by incorrect usage and cultural confusion. When you boil knowledge down to 140 characters (which was a requirement of the original version of the social medium Twitter [now called "X"]), or what one click on a web page can emote, you fall miserably short of the intent. Two of my favorite speeches are Abraham Lincoln's Gettysburg Address and Martin Luther King's "I Have a Dream" speech. Both are brief in the annals of great discourse, with Lincoln's 275 words taking less than 2 minutes to recite and King's speech lasting about 17 minutes, but to characterize either with a soundbite is woefully incomplete. Take this excerpt from Dr. King's speech:

"And when this happens, and when we allow freedom to ring, when we let it ring from every village and every hamlet, from every state and every city, we will be able to speed up that day when all of God's children, black men and white men, Jews and Gentiles, Protestants and Catholics, will be able to join hands and sing in the words of the old Negro spiritual: "Free at last! Free at last! Thank God Almighty, we are free at last!"

Those are powerful words. The "free at last" rhetoric at the end is the audible stamp and call to action. But, what action? The final paragraph starts with "And when this happens." You have to have listened to or read the previous 16 minutes to understand what the "this" is. If you don't know the "this," then, you're left with a rallying cry to an emotion that has no mission behind the vision. If you clip "I Have a Dream" to something quaint or cute like today's influencers would use, you're left with the "I Have a Thought" speech. We've substituted the *thought* of leadership for *actual* leadership. Here are some of the ways we're settling for less.

Smart or Subject Matter Expert (SME)

As the title would imply, a subject matter expert is someone who has a unique insight into a specific area. They have knowledge, credibility, and evaluated success in their field or craft. Their performance is superior; they are the "best of the best." When I have a problem with my automobile, I contact my friends at The Tire Depot, because they've proven they are SMEs in the area of fixing my car. If my house needs a repair that is beyond my capabilities, I'll call my friends Rod Cadenhead, Tim Dukes, or Royd Walker, because they can fix anything. If I have medical questions, I'll call upon the expertise of my daughter, Kate, who is a nurse, or my sister-in-law Susan, who is a doctor.

On August 2, 1990, Saddam Hussein ordered his Iraqi Army and Air Forces to launch an invasion into Kuwait. The United States and several coalition partners responded with a massive build-up code-named OPERATION DESERT SHIELD. As political negotiations dragged on, U.S. military leaders took center stage. General Colin Powell was Chairman of the Joint Chiefs of Staff, General Norman Schwarzkopf was commander of United States Central Command (CENTCOM) and had responsibility over forces in the region, and General Chuck Horner oversaw all aerial forces. With no diplomatic resolution in sight, coalition forces launched OPERATION DESERT STORM on January 17, 1991. Five weeks of aerial bombardment were followed by a ground assault on February 24. One hundred hours later, there was a ceasefire as the U.S.-led invasion moved with devastating speed and efficiency to remove Iraqi troops from Kuwait. Praise was heaped on the commanding generals Powell, Schwarzkopf, and Horner. The Army received appropriate acknowledgment for their sterling efforts. However, it was a little-known SME who made it all possible.

Air Force Colonel Jack Warden was a combat veteran. He flew F4 Phantoms and OV-10 Broncos in Vietnam in the late 1960s. He had a tour at the Pentagon in the late 1970s, working in the plans division. After several other operational assignments for various fighter wings, Warden found himself back at the Pentagon in 1989. He was widely considered the premier air strategist in the military. As he started his second headquarters stint, he dusted off a Soviet-era think tank called Checkmate and began to look at air-battle doctrine from a fresh perspective, paying specific emphasis to world trouble spots. Following the Iraqi invasion of Kuwait, Schwarzkopf called the Pentagon and asked that planners assemble a strategy to defend Saudi Arabia and defeat Saddam Hussein's forces. Already ahead of the request, Warden's team delivered the **"shock and awe"** campaign that was the key to victory. Author David Halberstam said in *War in a Time of Peace: Bush, Clinton and the Generals* said, ". . . if one of the news magazines had wanted to run on its cover the photograph of the man who had played the most critical role in achieving victory, it might well have chosen Warden instead of Powell or Schwarzkopf." Jack Warden is a subject matter expert.

Yet, being an expert in an area does not make you a leader in that or any other area. To be a leader, you need expertise in your area of responsibility, but expertise alone is not a singular qualifier. Leon Panetta was White House Chief of Staff, under President Bill Clinton, during my time with Air Force One. He later went on to serve as the Director of the Central Intelligence Agency. In the movie *Zero Dark Thirty*, actor James Gandolfini plays the role of Leon Panetta. In the movie, following a briefing about the potential whereabouts of Osama Bin Laden, someone comments to Gandolfini about how smart the person was who conducted the briefing. The actor responded exactly how Panetta would have said it, "Everyone is smart."

We've relegated leadership to a polished moniker of "he's smart," which is a baseless assessment that means absolutely nothing. If someone can deliver a fine speech or sermon, we anoint them as a great leader. Maybe they're just a good communicator but couldn't lead their way out of a paper bag. Someone launches a new business and it erupts onto the market, and we crown them the next guru of industry—when, in fact, maybe they just had a good idea for how to ship packages. Being a leader requires a level of industry expertise, but it also requires much more.

Talented

Some people are extremely talented. They might be musicians, painters, athletes, or preachers. There are gifted gardeners, writers, and accountants, but "talent" does not equate to "leadership." Talent in a field can be a precursor to one of the traits needed by a leader, but talent alone does not make someone a leader. We make continual errors in assessing people by calling a talented person "a leader." The evidence in this area is overwhelming. Hall of Fame basketball player Michael Jordan has had few peers when it comes to being a hoops player. The five-time National Basketball Association (NBA) league Most Valuable Player was a part of six NBA championship teams with the Chicago Bulls, in addition to a college championship while at the University of North Carolina. Yet, being a gifted basketball player has not translated into his ability to establish a leadership or winning culture as an NBA owner. He's rich and is a marketing phenomenon, but that doesn't place him in a pantheon of leadership. He and his representatives just know how to market him as a commodity. The same could be said for Andre Young, better known as Dr. Dre. He is an accomplished rapper, record producer, and entrepreneur. He runs a multi-million-dollar business, and that makes him an impressive businessman. It doesn't mean he's a leader. Jeff Bezos is the CEO and President of Amazon and one of the richest men in the world. He's gifted at making money, but being rich is a really poor quality for leadership.

John Maxwell saw the emerging flaw with overemphasizing talent exclusively when he wrote the book *Talent Is Never Enough.* Maxwell says, "The toughest thing about success is that you've got to keep on being a success. Talent is only a starting point in business. You've got to keep working that talent." He quotes the creator of Peanuts, Charles Schulz, who said, "Life is like a ten-speed bicycle. Most of us have gears we never use." Talent alone is only one gear of the leadership bicycle. Metaphorically, it takes all of the gear choices to properly navigate the journey laid out before you. Maxwell says leaders are *talent-plus* people. The thirteen traits of a *talent-plus* person are:

- Belief lifts your talent
- Passion energizes your talent
- Initiative activates your talent
- Focus directs your talent
- Preparation positions your talent
- Practice sharpens your talent
- Perseverance sustains your talent
- Courage tests your talent
- Teachability expands your talent
- Character protects your talent
- Relationships influence your talent
- Responsibility strengthens your talent
- Teamwork multiplies your talent

"One of the paradoxes of life is that the things that initially *make* you successful are rarely the things that *keep* you successful," says Maxwell. Talent is a fair catalyst for achievement, but it is a poor sustainment mechanism.

Organization and Management

What does your sock drawer look like? Is it neatly arranged, and are items positioned in a virtual Dewey decimal system of colors and styles? Some people have the ability to bring order to chaos. They might be the person in the class, on the playground, or in the office when a project emerges who organizes the group into teams, lines, or tasks. Yet, knowing that Religion belongs in the 200 series of books, and Literature is 800 doesn't correlate to awarding the label of "leader." Akin to the idea of organization is the label of "manager" or "supervisor." These terms are routinely viewed with disdain by people who fancy themselves as leaders. There are gifted supervisors and managers, and we need them. As a matter of fact, we've all served in those capacities at some point and will again. An organization will fail without individuals who can oversee people and tasks while ensuring the group continues to move toward its vision by living out its mission. However, just because someone is tasked with leading people or processes, it does not necessarily make them a leader. They may occupy the seat of a leader, but position alone is inadequate.

Marie Kondo knows a thing or two about organizing. The consultant, author, and television personality has made organizing your life an industry. She starred in the Netflix series *Tidying Up with Marie Kondo* and has written four books. In 2015, *TIME* magazine named her one of the "100 Most Influential People" in the world. If you want to categorize and sort your life, the KonMari method promises great results. Today's culture would call her a leader, because she is influential. Managing a process or bringing order to confusion doesn't make someone a leader any more than the student who has the responsibility of lining up their classmates for a trip to the lunchroom. Organization and management are valuable qualities for a leader, but they are side dishes to a main meal.

The misidentification of intelligence, talent, and organization and management skills as singular qualities of leadership does not mean those attributes are not important. They are vital elements which must be mixed with others to produce someone who is a leader. Additional aspects of the makeup of a leader include the following.

Sustainment

"Rapper's Delight." "My Sharona." "Brandy (You're a Fine Girl)." "I'm Too Sexy." "Come on, Eileen." According to VH1, those songs are the biggest one-hit wonders of all time. While you might recognize some of the titles, you would be hard pressed to name the artist of each song. Just as Right Said Fred, Dexy's Midnight Runners and Looking Glass didn't make a lasting impact on the music industry, a leader who enjoys only a singular moment of success or a lone avenue of accomplishment does not meet the standard of leadership. A leader is someone who can maintain excellence over a prolonged period of time. In Sam Walker's book *The Captain Class*, the author attempts to determine history's greatest sports teams and what made them great. One of the qualifiers was a winning culture, fostered by effective leadership. According to Walker, the Chicago Bulls teams of Michael Jordan didn't make the list, because they failed to sustain success beyond a singular group of people. Our society has migrated to celebrating and valuing the influencer, the overnight sensation, the thing that's hot now, and translating that to "leadership." Several years ago, there was actually a debate between the iPhone and Blackberry platforms. Some sports fans were passionate about whether a baseball player who used performance-enhancing drugs should be allowed into the Hall of Fame. The television show *Lost* captured a large market, and the actors were on everyone's "A" list. None of these hotly discussed subjects sustained the test of industry leadership. Our tendency is to let opinion polls and ratings define leadership. Polls might define preference, interest, and trends, but they are lousy at evaluating leadership and the value of sustainment.

The Dow Jones Industrial Average is a stock-market index that measures and tracks the performance of 30 large companies listed on stock exchanges in the United States. Formed in 1896, companies have come and gone as a part of this performance group. Sears and Bethlehem Steel were cornerstones for years but fell out of favor. General Electric has been a part of the DOW nearly without interruption since the index's inception. Raytheon Technologies was added in 2020 and wasn't even in existence during the first 50 years of the DOW's existence. The DOW is an easy example of how things go based on consumer need and want. Leadership, on the other hand, is more like a work of art. It may not be recognized or even appreciated in its time; however, it is eventually recognized because of what it produces: sustained excellence.

Diverse Achievement

William is a singer, a record producer of very diverse acts but also is an engineer who developed a piece of electronic equipment that he and his partner sold for more than $3 billion. Laurel started in the advertising industry. Then, she built her own multi-media organization and followed that up with starting her own investment company. Kevin played football and wasn't particularly noteworthy, but he used his experience to start an athletic-apparel company. He then expanded to develop fitness apps. Will I. Am, Laurel Touby, and Kevin Plank are people who have experienced success in diverse arenas. Leadership travels. There are some traits of leaders that are plug-and-play regardless of industry. Specialists may have success in a specific area due to a unique talent or a gifting of resources or rare opportunity, but leaders have the ability to move beyond a singular career to diverse avenues. John Glenn was a decorated military aviator and astronaut long before he started a career in politics in his fifties. Michael Bloomberg left his position as CEO of the financial software, data, and media company that carries his name at the age of fifty-nine to become a three-term mayor of New York City. Vera Wang was a successful figure skater and journalist before she became a premier women's designer. Media mogul Jonah Peretti was a middle-school teacher long before Buzzfeed became a household word. Leadership can navigate beyond the boundaries of talent, preference, and even success to go where no one has gone before.

Lief Babin graduated from the United States Naval Academy and served for thirteen years in the Navy. He held various leadership positions and is the recipient of the Silver Star, two Bronze Stars, and a Purple Heart. John "Jocko" Willink graduated from the University of San Diego and received his commission in the Navy. In his twenty-year career, he led at elite levels of the special-operations community, retiring as a Lieutenant Commander and receiving the Silver Star and Bronze Star with Valor. Following their military service, Babin and Willink co-founded Echelon Front, which is a leadership-consulting company. They've also authored several successful books on leadership. Babin and Willink were highly successful military officers and are now highly successful businessmen. They are highly respected and credible voices in the area of leadership development. And, they have achieved on various fronts. True leadership travels.

Multiplication

Part of the key to leadership sustainment is multiplication. Leaders make leaders. Some people make followers. Some make fans. Some make employees. Leaders make owners in the vision and mission, and this multiplication is a part of the leadership code. As of 2020, University of Alabama head football coach Nick Saban has had twenty-one former assistants hired as head football coaches in the collegiate and professional leagues. Certainly, the success of Saban's teams at Alabama has created the opportunity for his assistants, but his coaching tree pre-dates his time at Alabama. Saban was successful at Michigan State University and Louisiana State University prior to arriving in Tuscaloosa. At each of those stops, he developed a staff and multiplied his philosophy and style to others. Former head coaches like Lane Kiffin, Butch Davis, Mike Stoops, Major Applewhite, and Steve Sarkisian have opted to take a tour learning under Saban as an assistant or consultant rather than taking the next head-coaching opportunity offered. They see the value in his process of development and, specifically, multiplication.

When I arrived at the Mississippi Air National Guard in 1998, there was a commendable culture of leadership—but a vacuum of development. Due to some choices by members of the unit and the events of September 11, 2001, several of the presumed future leaders of the organization chose to retire or separate from the unit. This left a void of nearly two generations of future commanders. The raw material of leadership was in place, but it was going to require someone to assemble the parts and pieces and build for the future.

Major General William "Cris" Crisler put on his hard hat and went to work. Cris's philosophy was to invite people into an opportunity to observe how he led. Then, he would release you to practice those skills on a project, mission, or maybe a smaller command. Cris's own leadership résumé includes serving as a Squadron Commander on multiple occasions as well as the Vice and Wing Commander of the 172nd Airlift Wing, Chief of Staff of the Mississippi Air National Guard, and, ultimately, as Assistant Adjutant General of the Mississippi National Guard, retiring as a Major General. Cris's fingerprints of leadership continued to multiply as the unit's squadron, group, and wing commanders for the next several generations were part of his masterful development plan. Saying there is a lineage of great leadership is one thing, but proving it can be a taller task. Just because someone occupies the seat of leadership doesn't translate into organizational success. However, in the case of the 172nd Airlift Wing, they have a record of success to support their claim of success. They can boast of a safety record that is second to none, with accident-free flying surpassing more than sixty years. The numerous Air Force Outstanding Unit Awards bestowed to the wing were part of the reason the Air Force made the decision to outfit the unit with brand-new C-17 aircraft right off the assembly line and to designate the first Air National Guard unit to receive them. Leaders make leaders, and the 172nd Airlift Wing is an example of the key component of multiplication.

So, we overemphasize qualities like intelligence, talent, and the ability to supervise, and then we christen that as "leadership." We fail to properly evaluate legacy values such as sustainment, diverse achievement, and multiplication as essential elements of leadership. So, if we just make an exchange of these traits, will that suffice to create a healthy model and understanding? No. I think there's more.

The principal (not principle) reason for presenting this opinion is, hopefully, to elicit (not illicit) some perspective. We label people "leaders" far too often and far too early. Not everyone should get a trophy, and not everyone is a leader. Like some great artists, true leaders are more often recognized in retrospect, as most of the traits of leadership listed above take time to mature and properly evaluate. In the end, leadership shouldn't be about the title bestowed upon an individual but the impact made by the life that was led.

Over the next several pages, I'll introduce additional aspects of leadership that will form the concepts, character, and actions that I believe leaders embody. I learned these traits from my twenty-seven-plus years in the military, and I'll personify them with stories from that experience. Then, I'll outline how to employ that attribute in your life and organization. After retiring from the military, I embarked on a new journey as a pastor at a church. My application steps will directly address leading from this environment, but I believe the qualities I present transcend a specific occupation and are relevant to a mom or missionary, dad or dietician, pastor or principal, soldier, sailor, sales representative, or social worker. Greatness is available to you to lead in your home, school, business, community, and beyond. Learning how to lead yourself and, then, others is a vital component to that success. Let's apply some battle-tested characteristics to your life and trademark you as a leader.

CHAPTER 2

★★★★★★★

Integrity First; Honor Always

Integrity and honor are foundational to military service. They are fundamental to good order and discipline. Five-prime (5′) is the beginning of a DNA chain. Integrity and honor are the five-prime of a warrior. Every activity and action, each exercise and evaluation, all decisions, deployments, and determined operations hinge on the unbreakable decision of *integrity first and honor always.*

For the Air Force, the roots of these principles date back to the formation of the service in 1947. Concepts like accountability, dedication, and service were woven into the fabric of the life of an airman. In 1972, General John D. Ryan penned a letter to all Air Force personnel outlining the importance of integrity. He stated, "Integrity—which includes full and accurate disclosure—is the keystone of military service." He went on to say, "We may not compromise our integrity—our truthfulness. . . . Integrity is the most important responsibility of command." General Ronald Fogleman, Chief of Staff of the Air Force, formalized the service's core values in January 1995. "Service Before Self" speaks to a "we over me" commitment. "Excellence in all we do" is a call to ongoing improvement professionally and personally. The preeminent core value of the three fashioned by Fogleman is "integrity first." "An Airman is a person of integrity, courage, and conviction. They must be willing to control their impulses and exercise courage, honesty, and accountability in order to do what is right even when no one is looking," explains *Air Force Doctrine Publication 1.* Integrity is a code, a conviction. It is a decision as to how you live your life.

If integrity is the way you govern your life, honor is the way you treat others in response. The Greek Stoic philosopher Epictetus said, "Act your part with honor." Integrity is how you live, and honor is how you act. The understanding and adoption of this partnership is vital to becoming an Air Force officer.

My last assignment in the Air Force was from 2011 to 2013 at the Officer Training School (OTS) at Maxwell Air Force Base, Alabama. I arrived to serve as the Vice Commandant, the number-two guy, and had a stint as the Commandant during a transitional time of several months from the departure of one commander to the arrival of the next. OTS is one of three officer-commissioning branches of the Air Force with the other two being the United States Air Force Academy (USAFA) and the Reserve Officer Training Corps (ROTC). All three components are charged with the training and development of men and women in order to commission them as officers in the Air Force. OTS has a motto that states: "Always with Honor." There's a large granite sign with this inscription in bold letters by the parade field where trainees assemble for military formation and parade. It's positioned so that the trainees see it on Training Day 1 as they fall out for inspection the first morning of their life in the military, and it's the last thing they see as they take their commission and oath of office prior to leaving for their first assignment in the Air Force. In everything we do, honor. Let's take a closer look at integrity and honor separately.

Integrity First

"Integrity is doing the right thing, even when no one is watching."
—C. S. Lewis

"The time is always right to do what is right."
—Martin Luther King Jr.

"In matters of style, swim with the current;
in matters of principle, stand like a rock."
—Thomas Jefferson

"Waste no more time arguing what a good person should be. Be one."
—Marcus Aurelius

"Whoever is careless with the truth in small matters
cannot be trusted with important matters."
—Albert Einstein

"The strength of a nation derives from the integrity of the home."
—Confucius

"You are what you do, not what you say you'll do."
—Carl Jung

"If you tell the truth, you don't have to remember anything."
—Mark Twain

"The reputation of a thousand years may be determined
by the conduct of one hour."
—Japanese proverb

On March 16, 1968, Warrant Officer Hugh Thompson Jr., a U.S. Army helicopter pilot, and his two-man crew were flying a reconnaissance mission over the village of My Lai during the Vietnam War. They observed American ground troops killing unarmed Vietnamese civilians. Thompson landed his helicopter between the soldiers and the villagers, confronted the lieutenant in charge, and ordered his door-gunner to train the helicopter's machine gun on the U.S. troops if they continued to fire on civilians. He then radioed for help and personally evacuated survivors, including children, to safety. Thompson reported what he'd witnessed up the chain of command that same day, despite hostility and later backlash. Thompson acted with integrity.

What he reported became known as the My Lai Massacre. Estimates vary, but between 300 and 500 civilians were killed. Nearly every level of leadership attempted to bury Thompson's report. From the highest echelons of the U.S. Army, to the Department of Defense, to the White House, concerted efforts were made to cover up the report and the events at My Lai. Even after actions came to light, only Army 2nd Lieutenant William Calley was convicted of a crime. Calley was convicted of murdering 22 civilians. His sentence of life in prison was commuted by President Richard Nixon to three years of house arrest. No other military member or government official was held accountable.

Integrity is the foundation of trust, the quiet force that aligns actions with values even when no one is watching. It turns promises into commitments, power into responsibility, and short-term wins into lasting credibility. People and teams grounded in integrity make clearer decisions because they are guided by principles rather than pressure, convenience, or fear. Integrity also compounds over time. Consistent honesty, accountability, and fairness create reputations that open doors, strengthen relationships, and weather crises. In work and life, integrity is not just about avoiding wrongdoing; it is about actively doing what is right, especially when it is costly.

Integrity isn't always a dramatic stand against an overwhelming evil force. Integrity is sometimes a look, a pat on the shoulder, a question or a defusing statement. It's reviewing an expense report and saying, "I think you missed something" when you are confident it was missed deliberately. It's observing someone taking something and placing a hand on their shoulder and saying, "I believe you are more than that." Integrity is speaking up for someone who isn't in the room when a comment or joke is made at their expense. Integrity is returning or refunding the money. It's also admitting a mistake and attempting to reconcile the error.

Sometimes there are broader implications when integrity is tested.

- **Bottle to Throttle**. The aviation rule states a crew member cannot consume alcohol within eight hours of duty. It's commonly referred to as "8 hours bottle to throttle." One of my crew members violated that rule. The suggestions I received from the rest of the crew ranged from letting him fly with us but not allowing him to perform his duties, to leaving him behind but not reporting it, to saying he was too sick to fly. This advice was great if our duty was to protect the person. It was poor advice if we are called to accomplish the mission and steward the values of the Air Force. Since I was the person's commander, I reported the incident to my commander and told him my decision and subsequent punishment.

- **Government Documents.** Our unit was tasked with a last-minute mission. In an attempt to assemble a crew, a pilot approached me and volunteered. I reviewed his mission qualifications and discovered he had not completed all prescribed

> training. He handed me a training sheet, backdated the activity, and said he was "good to go." I pulled the pilot aside. I thanked him for his commitment to serve. I gently admonished him for what he did. He thought he was helping, but he was compromising his integrity as well as the entire unit's values. Some might applaud his efforts as selfless. Others would call it a felony and five years in prison for falsifying a government document.

Even in the somewhat benign situations above, doing the right, albeit hard, thing was not the initial response by some people. According to a 2024 Gallup Honesty and Ethics rating, a military officer was the third-most-trusted profession behind nurses and grade-school teachers. Yet, self-preservation, self-promotion, avoiding conflict, and personal relationships were influences with which the military officers above allowed to infect their integrity.

Tragically, leaders in the church have adopted the world's definition and practice of integrity. Unfortunately, the list below is not exhaustive.

- 2014. Mark Driscoll resigned as lead pastor at Mars Hill Church in Seattle, Washington, following numerous allegations of intimidation and bullying. Mars Hill had a weekly attendance of 12,000 with 15 locations in 4 states. Two years later, he launched Trinity Church in Scottsdale, Arizona.
- 2017. Ravi Zacharias, Christian Apologist, was accused of multiple acts of sexual misconduct and pattern of predatory behavior.
- 2018. Bill Hybels, pastor of Willow Creek Community Church outside of Chicago, Illinois, a church with a weekly attendance

in excess of 25,000, resigned amidst allegations of sexual misconduct.

- 2019. James MacDonald, pastor at Harvest Bible Chapel in Elgin, Illinois, with a weekly attendance of 13,000, was fired for inappropriate comments and financial mismanagement.
- 2020. Carl Lentz, pastor of Hillsong East Coast, often referred to as a "Pastor to the Stars," was fired due to moral failures.
- 2022. Matt Chandler, pastor of The Village Church in Dallas, Texas, took a leave of absence but was not terminated following revelations of exchanging inappropriate communications with a woman from his congregation.
- 2025. Robert Morris, pastor of Gateway Church in Dallas, Texas, a congregation of 30,000, resigned due to child sexual-abuse allegations. Morris, in turn, sued the church.

In a survey I conducted of staff and volunteers from 50 churches around the country, every respondent said integrity was the most important quality of a leader. When asked what position in the church was least likely to be held accountable for a leadership failure, all but one person said the lead pastor was likely not to be answerable for their actions.

These men's in-pulpit and public image was in contrast to their actions out of the spotlight. They lacked integrity. While these examples might grab the headlines, they are far from isolated. Leaders in the church are continually justifying their actions. This is akin to what is observed in the rest of society. Unethical business practices are rationalized as "That's just the way it's done." "If you want to get ahead, you have to be willing to do anything," implying that all actions are negotiable. The world and many leaders in the church endorse situational integrity. God's standards are not negotiable. They are clear and absolute—*not situational.*

In many vocations, discovering someone is untrustworthy is disappointing but manageable. You find another advisor, another vendor, another professional. Yet when a pastor proves untrustworthy, the harm ripples far beyond one relationship. A shepherd's character is read as a commentary on the message they proclaim, and the wounds of betrayal can harden into skepticism about the gospel itself. This is the tragedy of a minister without integrity: personal failure becomes public stumbling, and the credibility of a sacred trust is compromised, not only for a moment but for years, for many followers. In the words of Jesus in Matthew 5:37 and repeated by James in chapter five, verse twelve of that book, "Let your yes be yes, and your no be no."

If you want to move toward being a person of integrity, you must first consider this move as a decision that is followed by decisions. You have to make a commitment to live by the creed, and, then, you have to live it every day. Be prepared to be attacked for this stand. Jesus said that Satan is a liar and murderer (John 8:44). Being a person of integrity is a threat to Satan's plan to destroy. One of the devil's schemes is to isolate you or at least convince you that you are alone and, therefore, wrong. We can see through that lie in John 14:18, where Jesus said He would "never leave or forsake us." Truth that supports integrity will always overwhelm dishonesty.

A quality that supercharges integrity is patience. Patience reinforces integrity. Here are a few points that show that they go hand in hand.

- Integrity means acting according to your values even when it costs you. Patience creates the space to do that, especially under pressure.

- Patience keeps you from cutting corners. When outcomes are delayed, impatience invites shortcuts; patience helps you stay honest and thorough.
- Patience improves judgment. Waiting to gather facts and to hear others out prevents reactive decisions that can compromise ethics.
- Patience protects commitments. Sticking with promises over time—through setbacks and slow progress—is integrity in practice.
- Patience builds trust. Consistent, steady behavior over time lets others verify that your words and actions align.

In short: patience is the tempo that allows integrity to hold its shape over time, especially when speed, stress, or convenience tempts you to do otherwise.

Honor Always

During my time at Officer Training School, I was tasked with providing leadership to the staff, which included flight commanders, who were the primary instructors for the trainees, as well as other staff members who were specially trained in drill and ceremony, general combat skills, and physical fitness. If you've seen movies about basic military training, OTS is a cousin to that depiction. There is a combination of field and classroom training, as well as assembly-hall-type lectures. The lecture series is intended to be more inspirational than informational. The course is difficult, and introducing a motivational speaker is a way of rallying and encouraging the trainees; it provides a balance to the intensity of the program. In 2012, I invited Colonel Leo Thorsness (USAF, Retired) to come and speak.

Colonel Thorsness served in the Air Force for twenty-two years. He originally enlisted in 1951, at the age of nineteen. He was commissioned and completed pilot training in 1954. He flew the F-85, F-100, and, eventually, the F-105 aircraft. As an F-105 pilot in the Vietnam War, his primary mission was low-level interdiction such as bombing surface-to-air missile (SAM) sites, but he also had success in an air-to-air role, defeating other fighters. His speech to the trainees that day described the events of April 19, 1967, when he led a flight of four F-105s on a SAM-suppression mission near Hanoi, North Vietnam. Their task was to bomb these SAM sites, which would make it safer for other U.S. aircraft to fly over the area. Hanoi was heavily guarded with SAM sites, anti-aircraft batteries (AAA), and Soviet-made MIG aircraft, often flown by Russian pilots.

The flight divided into two elements, with two planes heading north of the city and the other pair focusing on the south. Thorsness led the southern formation, and, on their first run, they successfully destroyed a SAM site. During an ensuing run, Thorsness's wingman was hit by anti-aircraft fire, forcing the two crew members to eject. Simultaneously, the other two aircraft were engaged by MIG-17s. One of the F-105s experienced a maintenance problem, forcing the two aircraft to disengage from the fight and return to base, leaving Thorsness's plane, call sign "Kingfish 01," alone.

Thorsness and Electronic Warfare Officer Harold Johnson, who occupied the back seat of Kingfish 01, flew around the descending parachutes of the crew who had just ejected from their disabled aircraft. One MIG-17 approached the parachutes, attempting to strafe the men. Thorsness engaged that plane and shot it down. As a second and third MIG approached, Thorsness was low on fuel. He led the attacking planes away from the helpless airmen and outran them to a KC-135 tanker, where he was able to refuel and get back into the fight.

By now, the two airmen had landed, and recovery operations were underway. Two A1-E aircraft flew to the area to identify exactly where the downed crew were located, and an HH-53 helicopter was on standby, ready to fly to the area and retrieve the airmen. The two A1-Es came under attack from additional MIGs that had now arrived on the scene. One of the A1-Es had already been shot down, and the other was attempting to evade when Thorsness arrived back on the scene. He continued to evade SAM and AAA fire for nearly an hour while keeping the A1-E and the downed airmen safe. Additional F-105s showed up to lend assistance, and they shot down two more MIGs. Out of ammunition and low on fuel again, Thorsness was headed back to the tanker aircraft when one of the other F-105s announced they were critically low on fuel. Thorsness directed the F-105 to the tanker, putting himself in peril again. Unable to reach the tanker, Thorsness diverted to Udorn Air Base. When he landed, the fuel tanks' gauges indicated "Empty."

Eleven days later, Thorsness returned from a morning mission over the Hanoi area of North Vietnam. When he landed back at the base, Thorsness had completed his 92nd mission, just eight missions short of finishing his tour of duty. While not scheduled to fly the afternoon sorties, Thorsness voluntarily listed himself as a spare or backup pilot in case he was needed. Due to a maintenance problem, Thorsness and Johnson were elevated to a primary crew. While flying a mission they were not scheduled to perform, they were shot down by a MIG-21 and ejected over North Vietnam. Rescue efforts failed, and both men were captured and taken to a prisoner-of-war camp. Thorsness spent the next six years in captivity and was released as part of Operation Homecoming on March 4, 1973.

As Thorsness relayed the stories of combat aviation and surviving captivity in the infamous Hanoi Hilton and Heartbreak Hotel prisoner-of-war camps, the trainees were captivated by every word. The 80-year-old spoke with a strong yet unassuming voice. He stood 5'8" and was an athletic 150 pounds. His white hair was closely cropped, and he was always generous with a smile. His kind, gentle manner disarmed those around him so much that you almost didn't notice the Medal of Honor draped around his neck.

For his bravery during the mission on April 11, Thorsness was awarded the Medal of Honor. The citation reads:

"For conspicuous gallantry and intrepidity in action at the risk of his life above and beyond the call of duty . . . Lt. Col. Thorsness's extraordinary heroism, self-sacrifice, and personal bravery, involving conspicuous risk of life, were in the highest traditions of the military service, and have reflected great credit upon himself and the U.S. Air Force."

While Thorsness was awarded the medal for his actions in 1967, it was not announced until he was released, for fear of further torture and punishment while he was being held by the North Vietnamese. He was presented the medal in a ceremony at the White House by President Richard Nixon on October 15, 1973.

The Medal of Honor is the highest military decoration a U.S. serviceman can receive. No one "wins" the Medal of Honor. It is bestowed or awarded to an individual for acts of valor.

Thorsness's life modeled honor. He treated a general officer, an officer candidate, and a civilian employee with the same respect. Thorsness was the OTS's Honor Code personified: "We will not lie, steal, or cheat, nor tolerate among us anyone who does." Notice that the subject of the statement is plural and not singular. The commitment is that the entire school, from the Commandant, to the sergeant who works in the administrative section, to every trainee, collectively adhere to the code while helping their fellow airmen model it as well. It's not a *rule*. It's not a *policy*. It is a *character trait* we unite to live by. It's not used as leverage against someone who has compromised the solemn oath. It's a way to define who we are and who we will be.

By definition, "honor" means to have the highest regard in our thoughts about someone or something that translates into actions that show value. Honor is the act of paying respect. It's not the act of receiving, demanding, shouting, demonstrating, arguing, fighting, or killing in order to receive. Honor is designed to be given, presented, and offered without expectation of anything in return. By definition, it can't be earned, purchased, or demanded. It must be given. Society is trying to use honor in a way for which was not intended or designed. An object has a specific design. Let's take a spatula, for example. Time yourself for 30 seconds and name every use you can think of for a metal spatula.

Maybe you listed flipping over pancakes. You could have said to scrape ice off of your car windshield. Maybe you thought about using it as a straightedge to draw a line. You might use it as a cutting device, backscratcher (please wash after use), weapon, tongue depressor, or as something with which to remove gum from the bottom of a school desk. While you can use a spatula for all of those things, it's best to use it for its primary, intended design, which is to lift or spread things like food or drywall mud.

Objects are best used for their primary design, and subjects are likewise intended to be learned for a purpose. Let's take math, for example. You can learn it to pass a test, but the power behind math is taking the principles and applying them to your personal and professional life. Would you rather have 15% off a purchase of $1500 or $250 manufacturer's cash back on a $1500 purchase? If you're building a house and have a budget of $15,000 for flooring, and you're covering 1,500 square feet, can you afford flooring that is $11 per square foot?

If you hope to finish a class with a 90 average, and your current grade is an 88, what do you need to make on the final exam to secure your desired average, if the final counts for 50% of your total grade? You can merely learn formulas and pass a math test, but the design is to be able to apply the knowledge practically.

It's best if you use objects and subjects for their ultimate design. Principles must be used by their design and definition, or it can be deadly. For example, if you tried to live outside of the principle of gravity, it would be costly. If you walked onto the patio of the 50th-floor office of the Chrysler Building in New York and decided to jump, you would be dead in approximately 15 seconds (3 seconds per ~150 feet; 150 feet per 10 floors of a building. 5 x 10 floors = 50 floors. 3 seconds x 5 = 15 seconds). If you assume you're above the law when it comes to gravity, you will learn the error of your misuse of this principle. Just as gravity is a clear and unrefutable principle, honor carries similar undeniable characteristics.

If integrity is in short supply, then honor appears to be on back order. Based on the definition above, it stands to reason that, if honor is demanded, expected, or attempted to be extracted, severe consequences will result. Imagine the United States presidential election of 2020 if both candidates had extended honor. What would the momentum of race relations look like anywhere on our planet if we chose to honor without judgment or assumption? In Malcolm Gladwell's book *Talking with Strangers*, he recounts a 2015 traffic stop in Texas between Sandra Bland and police officer Brian Encinia. As you read the author's version of this event, you find yourself telling both participants to "stop," "take a breath," in hopes the situation will de-escalate. Bland eventually committed suicide in prison. If Bland and Encinia had used the principle of honor, this tragedy would have been avoided.

Our world has subscribed to a perverted use and practice of honor. Shouting for someone to extend honor is contradictory to its core use—that it must be offered as a gift. Marches and demonstrations by people who feel offended will never extract honor from those who are unwilling to grant it. Culturally, in the United States, we use the words "honor" and "respect" nearly interchangeably. Since the practice of our language equates these words, honor is further hijacked. People say, "You have to earn my respect," or, in other words, "You have to earn my honor." This statement and the ensuing value people place on it are completely wrong and further the dark practice of trying to steal, manipulate, or force someone to extend honor. A society that advocates take, not give; rule, not serve; revenge, not grace, is doomed to an incessant appetite of selfishness. The final result is a black hole of anger, bitterness, and loneliness. In *Honor's Reward: The Essential Virtue for Receiving God's Blessing*, author John Bevere writes, "Do we honor them for the extras? No, a thousand times no. We [honor them] because God gave us the charge to honor all."

The Bible has much to say on the subject of honor.

- 1 Samuel 2:30 (b): Those who honor me I will honor, but those who despise me will be disdained.
- 1 Peter 2:15–17: For such is the will of God, that by doing right you silence the ignorance of foolish people. Act as free people, and do not use your freedom as a covering for evil but use it as bond-servants of God. Honor all people, love the brotherhood, fear God, honor the king.
- Romans 12:10: Be devoted to one another in brotherly love; give preference to one another in honor.
- Exodus 20:12: Honor your father and your mother, so that your days may be prolonged on the land which the Lord your God gives you.

- Proverbs 3:9: Honor the Lord from your wealth, and from the first of all your produce.
- Psalm 91:15: He will call upon Me, and I will answer him; I will be with him in trouble; I will rescue him and honor him.

Our created design is to be people who honor one another. Our sin nature and the sinful surroundings of this world are screaming at us to go against our Designer. Satan whispers to us that we will be taken advantage of or miss out if we honor in such a manner. The irony is that, when we practice honor, we actually receive more than we give. Matthew 6:19–21 says, "Do not store up for yourselves treasures on earth, where moth and rust destroy, and where thieves break in and steal. But store up for yourselves treasures in heaven, where neither moth nor rust destroys, and where thieves do not break in or steal; for where your treasure is, there your heart will be also." God's economy teaches that we are richer in eternal things when we live as He designed us.

In addition to demanding honor, another way that leaders in the church are practitioners of the world's ideology is to whom deference is given. Honor is not reserved only for authority. It's not granted only to people we like or people who can help us advance. Honor is 360 degrees. We are to honor authority, peers, and those we oversee.

The Bible calls us to honor authority. Romans 13:1–7 says, "Every person is to be subject to the governing authorities. For there is no authority except from God, and those which exist are established by God. Therefore, whoever resists authority has opposed the ordinance of God; and they who have opposed will receive condemnation upon themselves. For rulers are not a cause of fear for good behavior, but for evil. Do you want to have no fear of authority? Do what is good and you will have praise from the same; for it is a servant of God to you for good. But if you do what is evil, be afraid; for it does not bear the sword for nothing; for it is a servant of God, an avenger who brings wrath on the one who practices evil. Therefore, it is necessary to be in subjection, not only because of wrath, but also for the sake of conscience. For because of this you also pay taxes, for rulers are servants of God, devoting themselves to this very thing. Pay to all what is due them: tax to whom tax is due; custom to whom custom; respect to whom respect; honor to whom honor."

When I worked for Air Force One from 1996 to 1998, Bill Clinton was president. While my political convictions differed from President Clinton's and some of his actions were character failures, I honored him in word and deed. When the president's inappropriate relationship became public in 1998, many people, including White House staffers, took the opportunity to criticize him. Clearly his actions were wrong, and we, as Christians, would call it "sin"; as a society, most would label it "immoral." In the midst of the controversy, I heard many people say they would "honor the office of the president, but not the man, Bill Clinton." Yet, by definition, by dishonoring Mr. Clinton, you have dishonored his office. Remember, honor means to have the highest regard in our thoughts about someone or something that translates into actions that show value. It would be impossible to truly honor the Office of the President of the United States while failing to give honor to the person who holds the office. Jesus had no reason to honor Pilate in John 18, nor the office which he held, except for the fact that it is the very character of God that He should honor.

We're also called to honor those beside us. This might be a co-worker, a sibling, a fellow patron at a restaurant or athletic event, or someone in the congregation with us at church. We should honor people who are beside us. Among our peers, culture likes to tell us to create a hierarchy. We place value based on talent, job title, money, and the appearance of a spouse. The car you drive and the neighborhood where you reside are insidious ways in which we create a structure that calls us to honor some more than others. We're willing to open our wallet and pay for the meal for a client, because that's the cost of doing business, and it's acceptable, but we brush by the senior citizen who is struggling with the menu or even how to pay without a thought of honoring them by helping and even paying for their meal.

Pashtunwali is the code of conduct for the Pashtun people. Their origins can be traced back to the grandson of King Saul of Israel, Afghana, who was born about 1,000 B.C. Many of the tribes of Afghana eventually moved to Southern and Central Asia, specifically between the Hindu Kush of northern Afghanistan and the Indus River in Pakistan. Today, the people commonly referred to as Afghans would trace their origins to the Pashtuns. Depending on your research, there are between nine and twelve components of Pashtunwali. Regardless of the list, there is a strong theme of honor that runs central to the creed. *Nang,* one of these elements, translates to dignity, esteem, or honor. It is a call to defend and stand up for those around you, particularly the weak. *Naamus* calls for men to stand up and defend the honor of women. *Nanawatai* was emphasized in the movie *Lone Survivor*, which tells the story of Navy Petty Officer First Class Marcus Luttrell. *Nanawatai* calls for the Pashtun people to provide safe haven and protection to anyone under their authority, which includes their tribal area around their home. *Hewaad* is the concept of protecting and honoring the land, culture, and your fellow citizens.

During my many tours in Afghanistan from 2002 to 2013, I observed this code firsthand. It was more than conduct; it went deeper. It was the very essence of these people. It was so ingrained in them and modeled by them that there's no concept of life another way. In other words, it was a principle, like gravity, that would be impossible to violate. Rather than focusing on our differences with the Afghani people, maybe we could step toward their principle and practice of honoring those beside us.

One of the most important leadership lessons and practices is to know how to honor those you oversee. There is a biblical construct for this in 1 Peter 5:1–4, "Therefore, I urge elders among you, as your fellow elder and a witness of the sufferings of Christ, and one who is also a fellow partaker of the glory that is to be revealed: shepherd the flock of God among you, exercising oversight, not under compulsion but voluntarily, according to the will of God; and not with greed but with eagerness; nor yet as domineering over those assigned to your care, but by proving to be examples to the flock. And when the Chief Shepherd appears, you will receive the unfading crown of glory."

As with honoring our leaders and our peers, culture is issuing a different message when it comes to how you honor those you oversee. Concepts like transparency, honesty, inclusion, selflessness, vulnerability, support, and protection are cast aside for seeking an advantage, suppressing, demeaning, degrading, and selfishly seeking personal recognition and glory at the expense of others. The first way creates a culture of trust, commitment, and life. The second breeds toxicity, distrust, and death.

Colonel Tom Coglitore, call sign "Riddler," was an outstanding Air Force officer. For twenty-seven years, Riddler defined excellence, whether he was flying F-15Cs, serving as an instructor pilot on that weapons system, overseeing the implementation of the F-22 and F-35 programs, Commanding the Officer Training School (OTS) or serving as Director, Air Superiority Core Functional Team. When you think "fighter pilot," you don't need to imagine a fictional character like Pete "Maverick" Mitchell in the movie *Top Gun*. You can think of Riddler Coglitore, who has actually done it. With a résumé and list of contacts like Riddler's, he could treat people any way he would like. Specifically, people he oversaw might even allow it just to have the prestige of saying they know him or work for him. But, Tom

Coglitore is a man of honor. You wouldn't notice a difference in the way he speaks to or treats an Airman Basic from the way he speaks to or treats the Air Force Chief of Staff. Tom is kind, humble, and a champion for others. I've known few men to deflect credit and heap praise on others more than him. Tom never forsook the responsibility of leading or commanding and wouldn't abdicate his duties, and he always sought ways to elevate others.

Knowing and understanding honor is one thing. The *act* of honoring is different. Information without transformation is useless. So, how do you honor?

- With your time. Not the leftovers of your time or at moments that are convenient for you. Give time sacrificially without bringing attention to the cost to you.
- By being curious about someone else's story. "Would you tell me more about that?"
- By showing courtesy and respect.
- By listening and hearing. "Could you help me understand what you mean?"
- By celebrating the success of others. "Congratulations." "Well done." "I'm proud of you."
- By serving first and going last. "After you." "May I help you?"

Jesus describes the posture of honor brilliantly in Luke 14:7–11. "Now He began telling a parable to the invited guests when He noticed how they had been picking out the places of honor at the table, saying to them, 'Whenever you are invited by someone to a wedding feast, do not take the place of honor, for someone more distinguished than you may have been invited by him, and the one who invited you both will come and say to you, 'Give your place to this person,' and then in disgrace you will proceed to occupy the last place. But whenever you are invited, go and take the last place, so that when the one who has invited you comes, he will say to you, 'Friend, move up higher'; then you will have honor in the sight of all who are dining at the table with you. For everyone who exalts himself will be humbled, and the one who humbles himself will be exalted."

In leadership, integrity grounds decisions in principle. Honor is the social credit and moral authority that follows, enabling others to entrust you with their effort, information, and well-being. Lose integrity, and honor becomes performance. Keep integrity, and honor becomes legacy.

Application

Give yourself an integrity and honor checkup. Look for patterns rather than singular incidents.

Honesty and Truth

- Do I tell the whole truth, even when a partial truth would be easier?
- Do I avoid exaggeration or convenient omissions?
- If I'm wrong, do I admit it quickly and clearly?

Promises and Follow-Through

- Do I keep commitments without needing reminders?
- When I can't keep a promise, do I take ownership and renegotiate early?

Accountability

- When I make a mistake, do I name it, fix it, and learn from it without deflecting or blaming?
- Do I accept consequences for my choices?

Consistency and Courage

- Are my actions aligned with my stated values when it's costly, inconvenient, or when no one is watching?
- Do I speak up respectfully when something is wrong, even if it risks approval or advantage?

Fairness and Respect

- Do I treat people with dignity, regardless of status, usefulness, or agreement with me?
- Do I give credit generously and avoid taking what isn't mine?

Boundaries and Conflicts of Interest

- Do I disclose conflicts and recuse myself when needed?
- Do I avoid using insider information or relationships for unfair gain?

Transparency and Motives

- Would I be comfortable if my reasons and actions were made public to those affected?
- Am I willing to explain my decisions to those who bear the impact?

Empathy and Impact

- Do I consider how my choices affect those with less power or voice?
- When I benefit, do I ensure I'm not quietly shifting costs onto others?

Stewardship

- Do I take care of resources (money, time, data, environment) as if they were my own—and, when they are my own, as if they were entrusted to me?

Humility and Growth

- Do I invite feedback, change my mind with new evidence, and apologize well?
- Do I practice the values I expect from others?

Private vs. Public Self

- Is the person I am in private consistent with who I appear to be in public?
- Do I avoid rationalizations like "Everyone does it" or "It's just this once"?

Law, Policy, and Conscience

- Do I meet the legal standard—and, when legal isn't ethical, do I choose the ethical?
- Do I follow policies even when enforcement is unlikely?

Digital Integrity

- Do I behave online (emails, texts, posts) with the same honesty and respect I aim for in person?

Long-Term Lens

- If my future self looked back, would they be proud of this choice?
- Would I be comfortable if someone I mentor or my children copied my behavior?

How to Use This

- Invite three people into these questions. Ask them to write their answers. Then, meet in-person to discuss.
- Pick three to five questions that hit a nerve, and journal on real situations from the past month.
- Identify one small, concrete behavior to improve this week.
- Revisit monthly, and look for trendlines, not perfection. Integrity grows through consistent, honest course-correction.

CHAPTER 3

★★★★★★★

Commitment

I was sitting on a concrete floor wearing a pair of shorts, a T-shirt, combat boots, and socks, and I was soaking wet. The floor was cold, and I was in a small space approximately 24 inches by 18 inches with a height of 36 inches. I'm 5'10" and weigh 180 pounds. My frame was squeezed into this spot with assistance. The side of this plywood container had holes. I'll explain the purpose of the holes later. There was heavy-metal music blaring over the loudspeakers. The volume was so great the sound waves felt like they were pressing against my body. The lights in the room were intense and would pierce through the holes and crevices of my tiny home. I'm not sure how long I had been in the box this time. After being sleep deprived for a week, your mind begins to struggle. According to WebMD, "Lack of sleep hurts the cognitive processes in many ways. First, it impairs attention, alertness, concentration, reasoning, and problem-solving. This makes it more difficult to learn efficiently. Second, during the night, various sleep cycles play a role in 'consolidating' memories in the mind. If you don't get enough sleep, you won't be able to remember what you learned and experienced during the day." I had no idea what time of day it was or even day of the week.

I closed my eyes with a vain hope that I could sleep, but it was impossible. I heard voices and the sound of footsteps approach—even over the sound of the music. Then, things got a little more intense. Someone was taking an object and banging on the side of the container that held me. If you ever wonder whether you want to be the hammer or the nail, trust me, you want to be the hammer. The people outside of my container—three, according to my count—took turns beating the sides and top of the box until they got tired and passed the bat or golf club or long lead pipe to the next person for their turn. This went on for a while. With each blow, the crate would shake, and I wondered how much more it could take until it gave way to the force of the blows. Even though I was so tightly squeezed inside this box, every time there was a "Bam" against it, I found my body naturally reacted in a defensive mode. My muscles would tighten, I would try to lower my head even deeper between my knees, and I would pull my legs together even closer in an attempt to stave off the blow in case it came crashing through the plywood.

The blows stopped. Maybe they got tired. I could feel my heart racing. My head was throbbing. Despite the cool temps and my damp clothes, I could feel a cold sweat. Then, I felt a pain in my right side near my kidney. Next, a shot to the lower back. Then, a stab to the right shoulder. The guards had decided to stop whacking the box and instead opted to shove the instrument through the holes in the box. It was a game of "human whack-a-mole." Each of the three men had a long stick or pole. They would take turns shoving it inside one of the holes until it made contact with my body somewhere. They would poke me from one side, which forced my body to react in the direction of the spare one or two inches of the box, only to be struck immediately by another guard who was prepared to take advantage of my adjustment and inflict some pain and discomfort in a different bodily area. I'll give it to these guys—they were good. They knew just how to choreograph their moves perfectly to increase my anxiety and confuse my mind. This went on for several minutes before ending. I was gasping for air. Even though the box wasn't airtight, I guess my anxiousness was causing me to gasp for air.

Sometime later, the same three guards approached my box and opened it. I knew it was the same guards because of their boots and their voices. They dragged me out of the box and forced me to stand. A slight breeze was coming through the building, which instantly made me shiver. I could see my breath, and the guards had on coats, so I'm guessing it was close to freezing. Next, they "encouraged me" to take off my shoes and socks. It's strange how much more vulnerable you feel when you don't have shoes on in a situation like I was facing. With my feet now in direct contact with the concrete floor, my body felt even colder. As I stood there, I heard a commotion. Three more guards, wearing black hoods, as all the guards were, came dragging someone just in front of me. She was similarly dressed in a T-shirt, shorts, and no shoes. She didn't appear wet, like me, but her hair was matted from dirt and sweat. Her head was low, and she was looking at the floor.

"Lieutenant, if you don't tell me what I want to know, I'm going to beat her." "Her" was a member of my team, call sign "Bambi." During their game of beat the box with me inside, they were asking for information about our unit and mission. I was not willing to surrender this information. They tried other tactics earlier that included temperature extremes, the use of ice-cold water to loosen my tongue. They hung me from a beam and held me uncomfortably close to an open flame and a hot poker. So far, I had resisted. Now, they were going to see how committed I was to my oath, our mission, and our country by giving me a front-row seat at them punishing Bambi for my lack of compliance. They took her back around the corner, and the screaming began. I'd hear a whack or a thud and, then, a scream.

It lasted for an eternity. Then, Bambi began to beg them to stop and called on me to help her. The best way for me to help her, to help all of us being held captive, was to uphold Article IV of the United States Armed Forces Code of Conduct, "If I become a prisoner of war, I will keep faith with my fellow prisoners. I will give no information or take part in any action which might be harmful to my comrades. If I am senior, I will take command. If not, I will obey the lawful orders of those appointed over me and will back them up in every way."

This routine continued for the next several hours and days. Then, in a daring raid, we were liberated from captivity. A team of combined U.S. Army, Navy, and Air Force operatives captured the camp and rescued us. It wasn't a long drive back to freedom. It was actually just a bus ride from the training area near Fairchild Air Force Base, Washington, just west of Spokane, to the barracks where we were housed for Survival, Evasion, Resistance, and Escape (SERE) school. The resistance and escape phase are conducted in a mocked-up prisoner-of-war camp that seems artificial and staged at first, and, as your fatigue and hunger increase, you wonder how make-believe it is. The training was stellar and prepared me for many circumstances in life, from the military, to personal, to other professions. The lingering lesson that marked me from that day or night that Bambi was being beaten was that I'd made a commitment etched in the words of the Code of Conduct but written in the blood of men and women. (She actually wasn't being beaten. Their sleight-of-hand of moving her out of my sight, but making the sounds all too real with the guards hitting a padded area by her, and telling her to scream was enough to convince my tired mind that it might be real). It is bigger than me, and I will not fail in keeping it.

Commitment today seems more like a convenience than a character choice. It's the punchline by someone who wants to degrade your beliefs. Commitment is mocked. It's antiquated. It's not open-minded.

It's circumstantial. Commitment is appreciated until something perceived to be better comes along, or a challenge arises that makes quitting appetizing. Ralph Waldo Emerson said, "Sow a thought, and you reap an action; sow an act, and you reap a habit; sow a habit, and you reap a character; sow a character, and you reap a destiny." When you begin to sow a thought of quitting, you're only an action step away from forgoing your commitment. And, when you do that, the stain runs deep. General Douglas MacArthur said, "Age wrinkles the body; quitting wrinkles the soul."

Part of the challenge in keeping a commitment is that, too often, we focus on don'ts. We make statements like "Don't quit," "Don't think about failure," "Don't go alone." By allowing these negative thoughts to even enter our mind, it means we are repeatedly contemplating compromise. If I say to myself, "Don't quit," during a training run for a marathon, I've allowed the thought of quitting to reside in my mind. Making a commitment is about saying "yes" to something rather than "no" to other things. This change of focus imparts positive thoughts. It's better to concentrate on what I'm pursuing rather than on what I'm trying to outrun. Here's what I mean.

Start something over stopping something. I ran my first marathon in 1998 in Birmingham, Alabama. The Vulcan Marathon traversed through the hills of Birmingham and its surrounding communities. As I was crossing the "Mile 22" sign, I was spent. I started the race too fast for my determined pace in my rookie exuberance. The temperature was in the mid-50s, and, so, for a marathon, it was a bit higher than my liking. As I saw the "Mile 23" sign, I said to myself, "Don't quit." Even uttering the word seemed to make the next step harder. Within a few yards, I was walking and running. I crossed the finish line meeting two of my goals: finishing and doing so in less than 4 hours. However, my stretch goals wilted away after the "Mile 23" sign. It took me more than 37 minutes to cover the last 3.2 miles.

If I had slowed just a bit from my maintained pace and finished the last 3.2 miles in 27 minutes, I would have met even my top goal. I believe the error was reciting "Don't quit" rather than "Keep pushing," "Persevere," "I've got this," "I am going to succeed."

Captain Pete Van Hooser, USN (Ret) knows something about persevering. In a word, Pete's résumé as a special operator would place him in a Hall of Fame if the military pandered to individual accomplishments. Yet, his résumé isn't the most inspiring part of his story. During a training exercise, he suffered a compound fracture, shattering his leg so badly that doctors told him that he'd never walk again, much less run. It was a career-ending injury. But as a warrior, you are never out of the fight. He told the doctors if he couldn't run with the leg, he'd run without it. "Take my leg." His leg was fitted with a prosthetic, and he would join in the most grueling runs with SEAL trainees. He even had a fin fitted to a different prosthetic, so he could complete grueling ocean swims that 99 percent of the world couldn't complete with two good legs, much less with one. Pete sustained, persevered, and even thrived.

Why is it so hard for people to keep their commitments? Marriage is a commitment, but in the United States, approximately 50 percent of all marriages end in divorce. It appears that commitment to marriage is unaffected by a person's faith decision. While divorce among church attendees has decreased in recent years, according to the General Social Survey (GSS), it still hovers close to the average of people who express no faith allegiance. I doubt that people approach marriage intending to divorce, but if all they are armed with is what society tells them about marriage—or what's been modeled to them by their families—they have a horrible playbook for marital success.

Jenna and I enjoy facilitating pre-marital counseling. In nearly every couple we've taken through the process, either the bride or the groom comes from a divorced home. As they approach forming their own family, their strategy tends to be that they will *not* do what their parents did, rather than focus on the kind of union *they want* to form. Commitment starts with a vision for what you want to become or accomplish, rather than run from failure.

Important aspects and considerations while growing your commitment muscles include:

Commitment Is Contagious

When you place a premium on commitment, you inspire others to do the same. Teri Alesch is a sterling example of that. Teri was a C-141 aircraft commander when I arrived at Charleston AFB, South Carolina, as a very inexperienced co-pilot. Teri was relatively new to the position, and dedicated herself to the craft of being an excellent pilot as well as a superb leader for the entire crew. The mission we were tasked with flying included stops at Lajes Air Base (Azores) as well as Rota Air Base (Spain) and Sigonella Air Base (Italy).

Usually, the pilots would rotate flying each segment. Teri flew the first portion of the mission to Norfolk Air Force Base, Virginia. This meant I was on deck to fly from Norfolk to Lajes. The winds at Lajes are challenging. They are predominantly from the south or southwest and constant. If you think Chicago is the "Windy City" or it's breezy in Oklahoma, they're mild compared to Lajes. The weather forecast called for the winds to be 25 to 35 knots from a heading of 240 degrees. This meant whether we landed on Runway 15 or 33, we would have a difficult crosswind. The C-141 has a maximum-crosswind-landing limit of 30 knots. Since the landing was going to be difficult, and I was so inexperienced, I expected Teri to tell me that she would execute the landing. As a matter of fact, I was kind of hoping she would. But, that's not what transpired. While Teri was committed to her craft, she was also committed to my growth and development.

As I flew this portion of the mission, we continually received weather updates. The winds remained constant. Sometimes, they were gusting out of landing limits for the airplane, and, on other occasions, they were steady right at the maximum allowable. As I flew the approach to the field, we broke out of the clouds at about 2,000 feet above the ground, and I began to visually line the plane up on the runway. In order to safely fly and land in a crosswind, you have to "cross-control the airplane." In this case, we were landing on Runway 33, so the winds from 240 degrees were blowing from our left to our right.

With no wind, a pilot keeps the wings level and the nose straight toward the runway. In a crosswind, a pilot must hold the wing on the side of the wind down. This would normally induce a turn, but the wind actually holds the plane up and keeps it level. I was holding the left wing down. In order to keep the nose of the plane tracking toward the runway, I had to use the opposite-rudder input, meaning that my right foot was pushing on the rudder pedal. While difficult, crosswind controls are a part of the skill set. The problem occurs when the winds gust. So, the pilot is constantly adjusting the wing and the nose to match the ever-changing wind conditions.

While my approach and landing will not be an exhibit at the National Air and Space Museum, we safely made it onto the ground. I was too busy to look at Teri's face during the approach, but her voice showed confidence in me and command of the situation. It was a confidence-building moment for me as a pilot. It invigorated me to be absolutely committed to my career field as a pilot and taught me to be the kind of leader Teri was by trusting my team.

Commitment means new construction—not remodeling existing old habits

Construct a new model of commitment—don't just remodel the old design. Famed automaker Henry Ford said, "If you do what you've always done, you'll get what you've always got." Psychologists call it Observational Learning or Modeling. It is a "method of learning that consists of observing and modeling another individual's behavior, attitudes, or emotional expressions." Now, just because you observe a behavior doesn't necessarily mean you will imitate it; however, without a different example, our tendency is to replicate what we have seen. For many of us, our models are not great, and our environment and nature present challenges. When we construct a new model of commitment, we shouldn't use the scraps from the old house, and we don't want to use the blueprints of a broken spiritual nature. We need new construction.

If you're going to build a house, your first steps would involve picking a site and determining the preparation work that needs to be completed, while simultaneously finding an architect to draw the plans and a builder you want to oversee the project. In finding an architect and subsequently a builder, you're probably going to look for people who have produced products that you like. You might see house plans in a magazine that pique your interest, and you pursue that designer. Similarly, you might drive around your community and see homes constructed by a specific builder that mesh well with your taste. If you want to be a person who makes and keeps your commitments, you'll follow a similar pattern. Who do you know that embodies the qualities of discipline and commitment? When you look at the pattern of their life, do you observe characteristics you would want to adopt into your own life? If you can answer "yes" to these questions from your perspective, contact them, and ask if they would be willing to help you build your house. In your initial meeting and conversation about entering into this type of mentoring relationship, you should establish and agree to a framework. While you might have other components, the elements below are absolutes.

- Chemistry. You have to enjoy the relationship. That doesn't mean everything is easy and there are no moments of tension, but compatibility and likeability will help you stick. Here's a test: are you looking forward to meeting with them? You might not look forward to talking about past mistakes, but you feel a sense of positive expectation as you approach the time to talk.
- Honesty. Don't waste each other's time, both mentor and mentee, if you're not going to be honest. The mentor doesn't have all the answers, but they have some good practices. It's OK to say, "I don't know. Let's find out." The mentee desires to improve and probably impress the mentor, which might lead to qualifying and justifying actions. In the military, we would often say, "If the baby is ugly, call it an ugly baby." Don't put gravy on Spam and tell me it's country-fried steak. Honesty is part of the diet that commitment is built on.
- Priority. The meetings, the homework, and the follow-up must matter. Ironically, your commitment to maintain your mentoring schedule is one of the first steps to solid home construction. During a combat operation, it seems everything is a priority. Getting an intelligence update, news on a change in the weather forecast, a maintenance issue, team assignments, and physical and mental health are just a few of the things that battle for your attention. As H-Hour approaches, you begin to reduce the number of things that take priority over execution. I would tell my team, "If it's not broken, burning, or bleeding, save it for later." The time with your mentor matters; keep the things that infringe on it at bay.
- Location, Location, Location. Supposedly, the three most important parts of real estate are location, location, location.

Location matters in a mentoring context. First, I believe the mentor and the mentee need to physically meet in the same space. Zoom is a great tool, but I've experienced that the degree of separation from a computer screen to a meeting in person is all that is needed for the encounter to be pushed significantly off course. In aviation, there is navigation rule called the "60 to 1." It's a general rule of thumb that says if a pilot travels 60 nautical miles (NM) with a heading error of 1 degree, the aircraft will be 1NM off course. As you add speed, the error becomes even more pronounced. If you're on an airline flight from New York to London, takeoff to touchdown is about seven hours and some change. If you're flying at 480NM per hour and you're off heading by one degree, you'll end up missing London by a little more than 56 miles. Over Zoom, it's hard to detect slight posture changes, voice inflection, and body tension. Using a Zoom-like platform as your primary means to connect is settling for less. Next, the location where you meet is important. I love Chick-Fil-A and have had many meetings there; however, an environment like this offers a menu full of distractions. You see people you recognize and stop to chat. Something catches your attention, like a loud noise or someone laughing. Any distraction from the subject is diluting the quality of your time. Find a space that minimizes audible and visual confusion. The last element of location is to be prepared and present mentally and emotionally. You don't prepare for a big meeting when you walk into the boardroom. I spent more hours preparing for a mission than actually flying it. Spend time processing the last session, contemplating your actions, journaling about the progress, and noting questions to ask and observations to make. Invest more time outside of your meetings than the sessions actually last.

Pick community/comrades for good reasons—not just because you don't want to be alone

You've probably heard about the unbreakable bond that is formed by brothers and sisters in the military. There's a unifying quality that is indescribable when you serve together. Movies give you a glimpse of it. The *Band of Brothers* series is a must-watch. *Saving Private Ryan, Taking Chance,* and *We Were Soldiers* also offer a peek into the strong connection. There are literally hundreds of names and countless stories I could share that would solidify this point. It's important to share a couple to give you a strong understanding as to the absolute value of community.

When I left the active-duty Air Force in 1998 and transitioned to flying for Delta Airlines full-time and serving part-time in the Air National Guard, I met Allen Randall. He was a fellow member of the Mississippi Air National Guard's 172nd Airlift Wing. As a fellow crewmember, he was a loadmaster on C-141s and, then, C-17s. Allen's job was to ensure that the mission we were tasked with that day was safely and successfully accomplished. He might be responsible for loading cargo, which could entail pallets, ammunition, food, and other supplies. He might oversee the loading and securing of vehicles, from Presidential limos to Humvees to MRAPs (Mine-Resistant Ambush-Protected vehicle). He might support passengers we were transporting, from troops destined for a combat zone, to special operators we were supporting with airlift, to military families going to a new assignment.

Allen could also turn the back of the aircraft into a makeshift hospital, where we would carry doctors, nurses, technicians, and patients bound for treatment around the globe from Bagram, Afghanistan, to Balad, Iraq, to Landstuhl Regional Medical Center in Germany, to Brooke Army Medical Center in San Antonio, Texas. Sometimes Allen was responsible for the respectful transport of our fallen comrades, returning them to their families and military kin through Dover Air Force Base, Delaware, for the celebration of a life well lived.

The range of the type of missions Allen flew is a walk through recent military history. Operation Enduring Freedom, Iraqi Freedom, and Noble Eagle are on his résumé. He also flew missions supporting humanitarian relief for earthquakes, hurricanes, tsunamis, and volcanic eruptions. He was boots on the ground supporting relief efforts for a nuclear power-plant disaster, famine of heartbreaking toll, and medical relief for pandemics, long before anyone ever dreamed of COVID-19. CMSgt Allen Randall didn't just do these things and arrive in those locations. He performed in such a manner that set a standard for excellence that all recognized and appreciated but few could ever emulate. To list all his military decorations and awards would take its own chapter.

Allen is part of my inner circle. He knows the best parts of me and the dark portions of my soul. He's seen me do things that are now part of military citations on medals I've received, and he's seen me show my backside in my less-than-stellar moments. In a technical sense, on an organizational chart and in military chain-of-command, Allen worked for me on numerous occasions, but our friendship drew from a deeper place than lines on a page connecting bosses to subordinates. I can talk to Allen about anything. I can voice my frustrations with personnel. I can get his advice on an operation. I can confide doubts and fears without judgment. I can vet decisions I plan to make and receive wise counsel.

In one particular instance, the decision I had to make involved his future. A recent retirement had left the chief loadmaster position open in our squadron, the 183rd Airlift Squadron. As the commander, it was my responsibility to fill the role. The chief loadmaster was responsible for leading these highly trained crew members. He would make staffing decisions and speak to crew makeup. He would serve as counsel to me on decisions about hiring, discipline, promotion, as well as non-retaining someone and exiting them from the military. I thought the decision was easy. Allen was the best person for the job.

I met with him to inform him of my decision. Allen is extremely humble, so I expected no visible signs of excitement. I anticipated his usual, "Yes, Sir. I'll do my best." But, that's not what I got.

"I don't think that's the best decision," he said.

"Why not?" I replied.

Allen answered, "There's a guy that's a little more senior to me. He deserves a chance. The men respect him. He would be a great person to follow our previous chief."

"But I think *you* being chief is the right decision."

"The right decision is often not the best decision, based on timing. I believe my time will come, but the best, right decision is for you to select him."

Even when my hardest decisions involved something that affected Allen, he was there with insightful and selfless words. Allen understands commitment to a mission even at the cost of personal sacrifice.

Besides a professional bond, Allen was a stalwart for my family. He was one of the original "refrigerator people" for my wife, Jennabeth, and our girls, Abby and Kate. If I was going on a deployment, temporary duty assignment (TDY), or a training exercise, I would write Allen's name and telephone number on a piece of paper and put it on the refrigerator. My instructions were, "If you need anything, call Allen." If the car broke down, if there was a plumbing problem, if my pay gets messed up, or you need help at the base, Allen was one-stop shopping for Team Wiggins.

Allen was a professional confidant and a safety net for my family. He was also a pillar of the community. He's a friend who is loyal without judgment and cares enough not to leave you where he finds you. He has equal measures of encouragement and correction. Allen showed me truth and grace. Dr. Henry Cloud describes these truths as, "Grace is unbroken, uninterrupted, unearned, accepting relationship. It's the relational aspect. Truth is the structural aspect. Truth is the skeleton life hangs upon; it adds shape to everything in the universe. God's truth leads us to what is real, to what is accurate." In your community and with the comrades who are part of your commitment fortress, you need people who speak words of truth and grace.

Commitment is always doing the next right thing

Kendell Reinhardt and Ann Williams exemplify this. In 1957, nine African-American students attempted to attend Little Rock (Arkansas) Central High School. Three years earlier, the United States Supreme Court had struck down segregation in their ruling *Brown vs. Board of Education*. While active-duty and National Guard troops were deployed to keep order and allow the students to be admitted, they were never welcomed. Kendall and Ann wanted to do something about it. They committed to befriending Elizabeth Eckford, one of the nine. A simple act of walking with her to class was bold and caused them to be ostracized, but Reinhardt and Williams were committed. They displayed this quality by simply making a step in the right direction and following that step with another and then, another.

With this in mind, making a commitment to your parents, spouse, children, boss, or pastor all come with the same responsibility. If you tell someone you'll be by to pick them up at 9:00 a.m. but don't arrive until 10:00 a.m., you've not kept your commitment. If you tell your wife that you're home late because you got "caught up at the office" but were really delayed talking to someone at work about a football game, you're not living in truth. We justify big commitments and little commitments by the world's standards. Not coming home immediately, as I had told my spouse, is a little commitment. Paying my mortgage on time is a big commitment. Telling your child that you would play superheroes after dinner is a little commitment. Turning in a school project or work proposal on time is a big commitment.

If you want to keep the world's scorecard of commitment, you'll get what Henry Ford said above and get what you've always got. If you want to be known as a person who keeps their commitments, say "Yes" to something, develop a new model and design of commitment, and surround yourself with a community that is equal parts truth and grace.

Application

Commitment and follow-through review

- Pick three to five questions that sting a bit, and journal against specific commitments. Set simple weekly metrics: percent of commitments with clear scope, on-time milestone rate, number of renegotiations done before vs. after deadlines.
- Do a fifteen-minute Friday review: re-prioritize, renegotiate, and calendar the next week's top-three commitments.

Before I commit:

- Do I clearly understand what is being asked for, by when, and what "done" looks like?
- Do I confirm scope, success criteria, and dependencies in writing?
- Do I check my calendar, energy, and existing obligations before saying "Yes"?
- Am I the right person, or should I delegate or propose an alternative?

Prioritization and capacity

- Do I choose commitments based on importance, not just urgency?
- Do I choose commitments based on who asked the loudest, who I like, and who I want to impress?
- What will I de-prioritize to make room for this new "Yes"?

Planning and resourcing

- Do I break commitments into milestones, with dates and owners?
- Have I secured the resources, information, and access needed to deliver?
- Do I identify risks early and put simple mitigations in place?
- Do I execute and follow through well?
- Do I make steady, visible progress each week, not last-minute sprints?
- Do I protect focus time on my calendar to work on top commitments?
- Do I make myself accountable to others in the process?

Reliability and quality

- Are my deliverables on time, accurate, and at the agreed quality bar?
- Do I avoid overpromising to impress and instead underpromise and overdeliver?
- Would others describe me as predictable and dependable?

Boundaries and saying no

- Do I say "No" or "Not now" when capacity is full, and explain trade-offs?
- Do I avoid accepting "soft" commitments I'm unlikely to honor?
- Do I hold others to clear commitments without becoming adversarial?

Learning and improvement

- After misses, do I examine root causes and change my system, not just try harder?
- What recurring patterns lead me to slip: estimation, distractions, unclear scope?
- Do I track and review my commitments weekly to adjust early?

Impact on others

- Do my commitments enable others to meet theirs, or do I create bottlenecks?
- Do I deliver what is actually needed, not just what I planned to deliver?

CHAPTER 4

★★★★★★★

Discipline

Discipline is a loud word. The volume of this word is dependent on how we use it. For example, when it's used to describe the product of not meeting someone's expectations, it has a negative connotation. For a child who disobeys a parent, it can look like a timeout. For a teenager who talks back, they may have to surrender their cell phone or forfeit the car keys as punishment. For an employee who has failed to meet a goal or violated a principle, discipline could involve things like a letter of reprimand, a demotion, or the loss of salary.

For someone who is described as a "disciplinarian," it sounds a little more neutral than punishment for an egregious act. Usually, we like disciplinarians for *other people*. You like for the vice principal or even the principal to be a disciplinarian if you're a parent. We're fine with the athletic coach being a disciplinarian, as long as your team wins and your child gets to play to your satisfaction. We like a boss who rules by the rules as long as their attention is focused on others and not infringing upon our freedom or autonomy.

When discipline is used to describe a characteristic of an individual, it has a completely different sound. It carries a reframe of respect, admiration, and even envy. When someone is disciplined to exercise consistently, we acknowledge this as a positive trait. Similarly, someone who has a regimen for eating properly, or who lives with fiscal soundness, or reads and learns consistently is applauded for their strictness to their arena.

"Discipline" is a word commonly associated with the military. For the most part, it carries a positive connotation. It describes the bearing of an airman, sailor, or soldier. George Washington said, "Discipline is the soul of an army. It makes small numbers formidable; procures success to the weak, and esteem to all." There are even regulations in the services that define and describe the concept of discipline, such as Army Regulation 600–20. Chapter 4 of this document, *Military Discipline and Conduct*, states:

> "Military discipline is founded upon self-discipline, respect for properly constituted authority, and the embracing of the professional Army ethic with its supporting individual values. Military discipline will be developed by individual and group training to create a mental attitude resulting in proper conduct and prompt obedience to lawful military authority.
>
> "While military discipline is the result of effective training, it is affected by every feature of military life. It is manifested in individuals and units by cohesion, bonding, and a spirit of teamwork; by smartness of appearance and action; by cleanliness and maintenance of dress, equipment, and quarters; by deference to seniors and mutual respect between senior and subordinate personnel; by the prompt and willing execution of both the letter and the spirit of the legal orders of their lawful commanders; and by fairness, justice, and equity for all Soldiers, regardless of race, religion, color, gender, and national origin.

> "Commanders and other leaders will maintain discipline according to the policies of this chapter, applicable laws and regulations, and the orders of seniors."

My earliest introductions to discipline started at home. Many were of the loud variety but delivered with love. My parents, Iris and Leo Wiggins, loved me and my brother and sister enough to provide correction as needed. They also modeled discipline. Whether it was the discipline of an exemplary work ethic or the discipline to follow through on what they said, I saw a woman and a man who exemplified a lifestyle of discipline. The most impactful lessons about discipline were provided via a baseball field.

My Dad loved baseball. He played as he could as a child, but growing up in the Depression of the 1930s in Gastonia, North Carolina, meant everyone worked, and there was little time for extracurricular activities. Finances were an issue. After school, there were jobs to be performed, like working in his uncle's grocery store or in the Threads textile mill. Leo Wiggins was never one to complain, but you could see a sense of loss in his eyes and hear it in his voice when he talked about baseball. With that as the backdrop, when I showed an interest in the sport, my Dad instilled in me an appetite for discipline. When it came to throwing the ball, you have to follow through. As for hitting, proper balance and weight distribution were vital. As for catching, keep your eye on the ball, and cover the ball in your glove with your throwing hand. I played catcher, so routines that were common for me were repeated throws to second to prepare for a runner trying to steal second. There were hours of practice of using my body as a backstop to block a pitcher's errant throws. The catcher needs to be disciplined to hold his glove steady and frame the pitch to assist the pitcher in delivering an accurate throw, and assist the umpire in accurately assessing it as a ball or strike.

The training I received at Sumner Park in East Point, Georgia, produced results in other facets of my developing life. The voice of preparation—which sounded quite similar to my Dad's cadence—echoed through me. Homework done in a timely manner and early was normal. A Sunday School lesson completed with answers written in the book was not prescribed, because it was assumed. Room cleaned up, dog fed, cars washed, and lawn cut were parallel consequences of the learning that took place by hitting thousands of baseballs in a batting cage, until my body memorized the effort as if it were my DNA.

On April 21, 1987, I entered the United States Air Force—Officer Training School at the Medina Annex of Lackland Air Force Base, San Antonio, Texas. This is where my pottery of discipline was placed into a kiln.

Air Force Instruction 36-2903, Dress and Personal Appearance of Air Force Personnel is like a preface in the book of a disciplined life for an Airman.

The basic philosophy spelled out in the regulation states, "Pride in one's personal appearance and wearing the uniform greatly enhances the *esprit de corps* essential to an effective military force. Therefore, it is most important for all Airmen to maintain a high standard of dress and personal appearance. The five elements of this standard are neatness, cleanliness, safety, uniformity, and military image. The first four are absolute, objective criteria needed for the efficiency and well-being of the Air Force. The fifth, military image, is subjective, but necessary. Appearance in uniform is an important part of military image. Judgment on what is the proper image differs in and out of the military. The American public and its elected representatives draw certain conclusions on military effectiveness based on the image Airmen present. The image must instill public confidence and leave no doubt that Airmen live by a common standard and respond to military order and discipline. The image of a disciplined and committed

Airman is incompatible with the extreme, the unusual, and the fad. Every Airman has a responsibility to maintain an 'acceptable military image,' as well as the right, within limits, to express individuality through his or her appearance."

A wise trainee would attend to the basics of grooming standards before showing up for in-processing, known as "Training Day 0." This time is set aside to ensure enlistment paperwork is in proper order, medical records receive a final review, and some initial-issue equipment is distributed. Showing up on TD-0 and looking like you don't belong in the military is a strategy fraught with challenges. You can earn a nickname or special attention that will follow you for the ensuing weeks. The last thing a trainee needs is to be the pet project of a Training Instructor (TI). Clearly, being in training commences even before the clock starts.

In addition to personal standards, maintaining your dormitory room to proper code is part of the philosophy of discipline. If you're conscientious enough to keep your personal items in order, the strategy is that this will flow into your commitment to your craft as a military member. Socks are rolled in such a way as to produce a smile by the elastic in the top. T-Shirts were rolled to be smooth with no bulging edges. There should be no stray strings—affectionately known as "cables"—coming from any garment. Lint is a killer. The heels of shoes should be touching and laces tucked in. Beds were made with exacting detail. Bath towels folded in a certain manner. Bathrooms cleaned of every perceivable foreign object, including the smallest piece of hair. I guarantee the bathroom floor of a trainee's room or hallway is cleaner than any plate you've ever eaten a meal off of.

Drill and ceremony brought personal standards and the philosophy of order and standards to a singular set of skills. Saluting, marching, issuing commands, and working in unison are central discipline rituals that produce fruit long after you leave the confines of the training environment. A twenty-four-inch step, a cadence of one hundred to two hundred steps per minute, and the interval established between each maneuver are harbingers of the regimen you will need as a pilot, aircraft mechanic, or a tactical air-control party specialist (TAC P).

Thankfully, the lessons of discipline learned in boot camp did not involve aircraft traveling at 600 knots or a jet engine that would carry the lives of men and women on a plane. The instruction was provided in a laboratory, where, at worst, you faced elimination from the service, or, at best, you received "performance adjustment," resulting in failed inspections, loss of privileges, and always the opportunity to "Do it again, trainee."

During Training Day 1, I was offered the first of many opportunities to re-accomplish a task. Following a stirring wake-up call from our training instructors, we assembled outside of our rooms and marched to the parade field. We were welcomed to the United States Air Force. I was told I had the opportunity to join the best fighting force on the planet and the most lethal service ever assembled. Following the 0500 inspirational words, we marched off to breakfast. Meals were a leisure moment. We were afforded approximately 90 seconds to eat, return our dishes to the kitchen, and form up outside for our next activity. We were divided into groups. I was part of a group that would have our initial meeting with our flight commander.

Captain Frank McGuire was my flight commander. He was not issued a smile by the United States Air Force, so he didn't display one. He stood about 5'8" tall, jet-black hair, perfect posture and wore a uniform that appeared to have been painted on his slight frame. I knocked once on his door as regulations directed. He barked, "Enter," and I stepped into his office at the position of attention. The prescribed verbiage to follow was me stating, "OT Wiggins reporting as ordered." I'm not sure what I said, but it failed to meet Captain McGuire's expectations. He replied, "That's a demerit. Try again." Strike one.

I stepped outside his office, and attempted version two. Strike two. Strike three followed quickly, but unlike baseball, the pitcher just kept throwing fastballs, and I became adept at swinging and missing. After receiving seven demerits, I cracked the code. Actually, I heard a trainee in the next office down get it right, so I mimicked her actions.

Officer Training School (OTS) afforded me additional opportunities to learn the valuable lesson of discipline. My first Red Line or graded room inspection yielded so many discrepancies that burning all of my issued equipment and starting over seemed my only logical option. Academics and athletics offered fewer challenges, as the rote I learned from my parents paid significant dividends. Eventually, the demerits decreased. My performance improved such that I actually secured off-base privileges one weekend, which was a delight, since my wife, Jenna, had flown in from Atlanta to San Antonio. Discipline, rinse, and repeat altered my thought process and actions in such a way as to allow me to successfully graduate from OTS and be awarded my commission as a 2nd Lieutenant. This characteristic, instilled in me day and night in training, proved invaluable as my career continued.

In the aviation business, the term "checklist discipline" is common vernacular. Each phase of flight (takeoff, cruise, descent, landing) has a checklist. These documents contain minimum cues required for a trained crewmember to configure the aircraft for a specific phase of ground/flight operation. There are also checklists for emergency procedures as well as abnormal operations. The checklist is designed to be followed step-by-step in precise order. "Checklist discipline" is the term used to describe the absolute necessity of completing each step as prescribed before moving to the next cue or action. The Interior Safety Inspection for the Air Force's C-17 has 35 steps, with each step containing one to several sub-steps. The Before Takeoff and Lineup checklists, which are accomplished just prior to taking the runway and while on the runway for departure, have 23 steps with several sub-steps. Some checklist items are labeled "Boldface." These are emergency procedures that require the pilot to know the actions by memory in perfect sequential order. Emergency Engine Shutdown and Smoke and Fumes in the Cockpit are examples of these critical actions. In addition to the Emergency Engine Shutdown checklist, there are 37 other instances that would require a pilot to shut down an engine following the normal Engine Shutdown Checklist. This 19-step process doesn't require memorization but does necessitate familiarity to the degree that the checklist serves only as a guardrail and not a crutch.

Checklist discipline is useless if the pilot doesn't have the personal discipline to routinely study the aircraft technical manual. The Air Force prescribes training disciplines from simulators to training flights to academic tests and flight evaluations. Yet, those are the *minimum* standards. Who wants to fly with a pilot who is defining the minimum in discipline? My disciplined study routine involved picking an aircraft system every week and reading everything I could about it. One week it was hydraulics. Next, it was engines, followed by pneumatics. Normal and emergency procedures had their weeks of special attention as well. After I finished every system—and all normal and emergency procedures—I would adopt a "wash, rinse, and repeat" mindset.

Discipline is a valued trait in a baseball player. It is said that "Discipline is the bridge between your baseball goals and baseball success." In the military, discipline is just choosing between what you want *now* and what you want *most*. Likewise, it's an important characteristic in the life of a follower of Jesus. Too often, I've seen discipline admired but not pursued. Pursuit is key in body, mind, and spirit.

Cary Nieuwhof said there are five things that give Christians a bad name with unchurched people. They speak weird, pretend to be something they're not, being known for what they're against and not what they're for, being experts on things they're not experts on, and claiming privilege. Four of these five qualities have their roots in a lack of discipline.

Establishing and maintaining a regimen of physical health is part of the stewardship God expects of His people and, even more, of His shepherds. "Or do you not know that your body is a temple of the Holy Spirit within you, whom you have from God? You are not your own, for you were bought with a price. So, glorify God in your body," says 1 Corinthians 6:19–20. Paul continues in verse 27, stating, "But I discipline my body and keep it under control, lest after preaching to others I myself should be disqualified."

Kathleen M. Zelman, MPH, RD, LD, has served as director of nutrition for WebMD and is a contributor to *WebMD Magazine*. She said, "According to a recent study, very few adults actually meet the criteria for a healthy lifestyle. The study, published in the *Archives of Internal Medicine,* showed that only 3 percent of American adults got a perfect score on what the authors say are the 4 basic criteria for healthy living. Just 13.8 percent met 3 of the criteria; 34.2 percent met only 2 criteria. Women scored slightly better than men.

The major aspects of physical discipline and, thus, a healthy lifestyle, include physical activity, nutrition and diet, medical self-care, and rest and sleep. Dr. Edward Laskowski, co-Director of the Mayo Clinic's Sports Medicine Center encourages aerobic (150 minutes of moderate or 75 minutes of vigorous activity weekly) as well as strength training (using all major muscle groups twice per week) for the physical-activity portion. Henry and Richard Blackaby, in their book *Spiritual Leadership,* write, "Leaders need not become obsessed with physical fitness, but those who ignore health issues are ultimately choosing to be less effective over time than they could be. People who fail to care for their health risk having their leadership come to a premature end."

With respect to diet and nutrition, medical self-care is another component of body discipline. Steven Tew, of Intermountain Healthcare, cited that 92 percent of Americans feel it's crucial to see their family physician annually for a checkup, but only 45 million Americans actually do it. This lack of discipline can be catastrophic. The Centers for Disease Control and Prevention recommends that "regular health exams and tests can help find problems before they start." My wife, Jennabeth, noticed a mole over her right eyebrow was changing shape and color. She arranged an appointment with Dr. Miriam Shatley of Belle Meade Medical. The results of a biopsy revealed melanoma. This started her on a journey of surgery, followed by Interferon treatment. I believe God used prayer, Jennabeth's timely discipline to seek help, and the gifts He placed in people like Dr. Shatley and Dr. Natale Sheehan (Jenna's oncologist) as His way to provide healing. I understand God does not choose to heal everyone in this way or even on this side of heaven. I can only testify to what He did in our circumstance.

Getting adequate rest has always posed unique challenges for me. As a pilot in the Air Force, flying at all hours of the day and night was common. So, finding eight hours of uninterrupted sleep was rare. I'd fill in the gaps with naps when I could. A flight surgeon taught a class on physiology and aviation. As part of his lecture, he discussed sleep patterns. He provided a pointer to help us fall asleep that I still use today. He advised to take a hot shower as the start of a bedtime routine. He explained that raising your body temperature and then allowing it to drop as you exit the shower and towel off improves your temperature's circadian rhythm. He said it also helps your overall sleep quality.

This habit followed me into life as a pastor. I have found that limiting technology and establishing a bedtime window are helpful practices for me. Johns Hopkins sleep researcher Patrick Finan, Ph.D., cites a higher risk for depression, irritability, anxiety, forgetfulness, obesity, Type 2 diabetes, high blood pressure, and heart disease for people who are sleep deprived.

A healthy body should be complemented with a healthy mind. Neurologists say that your brain needs to be trained much like you train your body. The goal of brain training is to transform inactive brain cells into active ones. Routine activities don't stimulate new cell activity; brain training encourages new experiences that require attentive thought. Just like physical fitness, brain fitness requires targeted effort through repetition. New and stimulating experiences may occur as part of daily life, but many of us operate on autopilot more than we realize. Exercising the brain daily is central to great cognitive fitness.

In November 2018, we were at the beach for our annual Thanksgiving getaway. I spend time during that week to reflect on the year-to-date. I assessed that, when it came to the discipline of my mind, I was not meeting my expectations. This led to a goal in 2019 of enrolling in what I called "Scott Wiggins University." As a student in this school, I was going to commit my mind to learning more about my craft. Just as I studied an airplane technical manual earlier, I was going to hone my skills as a pastor. While always seeking improvement, I read my Bible daily and journaled about what God was teaching me; however, there were other deficiencies in my curriculum. I needed to grow as a leader. I needed greater depth and breadth in systematic theology. I needed to understand my culture, current events, and history more acutely. There are literally hundreds of switches, knobs, and buttons in a C-17 aircraft, and I knew the results of flipping, turning, and pushing every one of them. How could I approach my calling to ministry with less zeal, less professional acumen, and less discipline than piloting an airplane?

I set a goal to read 24 books a year in order to grow in various areas mentally. Scott Wiggins University had adjunct professors like

Sam Walker, Ben Malcolmson, Simon Sinek, Wayne Grudem, Ryan Holiday, Mark Batterson, James Clear, Warren Berger, Adam Grant, and others. I also interject a diet of fiction authors into my routine. I find this helps my imagination in my non-fiction life. People like Tom Clancy, Mark Greaney, Vince Flynn, and Harlan Coben add some spice to my reading. A zest for learning supercharges my passion to engage people in many facets of life. Each year, I employ the same goal of reading 24 books, and so far, I'm undefeated. Lailah Gifty Akita, author and founder of Smart Youth Volunteers Foundation, says it this way: "How could you renew your mind, if you never read? As we travel to new places, we gain new perspectives and renew our thinking." A disciplined mind can be a doorway to creating an open spirit.

There are numerous lists of spiritual disciplines. Most lists would include Bible reading (2 Timothy 3:16–17, Psalm 119:105); prayer (1 John 5:14–15, 2 Chronicles 6:21, Ephesians 1:18, 6:18); fasting (Acts 13:2, 14:23, Luke 2:37); worship (Jeremiah 20:13, Psalm 75:1, Exodus 20:2); Sabbath; (Exodus 20:8, Mark 2:27, Hebrews 4:9); service (Deuteronomy 15:11, Galatians 6:2, Hebrews 13:16); stewardship (Malachi 3:10, Proverbs 16:3, Titus 1:7); and fellowship (1 Thessalonians 5:11, Ecclesiastes 4:9–12, Proverbs 27:17). Just as with our body and mind, we need balance and a full menu to reach health. Routine reading and studying the Bible without consistently praying leaves a hole the Holy Spirit is designed to fill. Fellowship with your small group without serving others falls short of the model Jesus provided.

I thought I was grading out with a solid "B" in spiritual disciplines, but I realized I had an anemic prayer life. I was invited, as part of a group of people, to weekend prayer retreat. This group included members of our church staff, Elders and their spouses, and a few other key leaders. We took a deep dive into the spiritual discipline of prayer. We were guided through several movements of prayer. After about ninety minutes, the group leader instructed us to take a break.

A break? I thought we were done.

We came back from our intermission, and we prayed for several specific things for the next ninety minutes. As Jennabeth and I walked to our room. I realized I did not have a lifestyle that facilitated a discipline of prayer. When someone says we're going to pray for an hour, I wonder what am I going to do for about fifty minutes of that hour after praying for ten minutes. Prayer is mentioned sixty-eight times in the New Testament (KJV). There are twenty-five examples in the Gospels where Jesus prayed (NASB). Frequency alone would indicate that it's important. Circumstances would affirm its vital nature.

We are called to "pray without ceasing" (1 Thessalonians 5:17). Jesus showed us this practically. He prayed at his baptism (Luke 3:21–22). He prayed in the morning and at night (Mark 1:35–36 and Luke 6:12–13). He prayed before and after performing miracles (Matthew 14:23 and Luke 5:16). He prayed before preaching (Luke 11:1). He prayed before meals (Luke 24:30). His dying breath was a prayer (Luke 23:46).

Systematically reading the Bible is vital. God decided to reveal Himself to us through these divinely inspired words. It's one of two (prayer being the other one) direct conversations with our Creator. The internet is dotted with Bible-reading plans to help someone avoid random and disconnected reading of this sacred text. In addition to reading, I strongly encourage people to journal about what they read. The added step of writing down what you read, its context, and how it applies to your life engages multiple brain regions improving recall and increasing the likelihood of application.

"Sometimes when I open my Bible to read, a verse leaps off the page, and I know God is speaking to me. Sometimes, I read, and nothing seems to be illuminated. Sometimes, I pray and have the keen sense that He is listening to every word and will answer me.

Sometimes, when I pray, I have no awareness that He's anywhere around. Sometimes, when I go to church or draw aside for some quiet reflection, I have the overwhelming sense that Jesus is right beside me. At other times in the exact same settings, I have no conscious awareness of His presence at all. And I know by each experience—as I read my Bible and pray, work, and worship—that He is teaching me to live by FAITH, not by my feelings." Anne Graham Lotz, *The Magnificent Obsession*

As mentioned above, there are several other spiritual disciplines that are vital for health. Being a steward of God's gifts—tithing and giving—is a key exercise of faith. If you are not a giver, you're either declaring you don't trust God or you don't love Him more than your money.

If you want to be different, you have to do differently. In order to do differently, you need to commit and discipline yourself. Zig Ziglar added, "It was character that got us out of bed. Commitment that moved us to action. And, discipline that enabled us to follow through." The philosopher Seneca said, "Most powerful is he who has himself in his own power."

Application

Complete the self-audit below. Pick three to five questions that sting, and journal one paragraph each. Choose one keystone habit to practice daily for two weeks. Do a fifteen-minute weekly reset: review metrics, refine priorities, and calendar the next steps.

Clarity and priorities

- Do I define a small set of top priorities each week and each day?
- Do I decide what *not* to do before I start?

Planning and structure

- Do I plan my week on the calendar, not just in my head?
- Do I break important goals into clear, time-bound steps?

Consistent execution

- Do I start on time and work the plan, even when I don't feel like it?
- Do I finish what I start before switching tasks?
- Do my emotions inform me, or do they determine my actions?

Focus and attention

- Can I work deeply for sixty to ninety minutes without electronic distractions?
- Do I control interruptions with blocks, statuses, or boundaries?

Habits and routines

- Do I have daily and weekly routines that run without motivation?
- When routines are disrupted, do I reset quickly the next day?

Self-control

- Do I delay short-term gratification to protect long-term gains?
- When I notice avoidance, do I take one small step instead of rationalizing?

Follow-through and standards

- Do I hold myself to a quality bar without perfectionism stalling me?
- Do I close the loop on commitments without needing external pressure?

Energy and recovery

- Do I protect sleep, movement, and nutrition to keep steady energy?
- Do I schedule recovery so I don't rely on willpower alone?

Accountability and measurement

- Do I track a few key metrics weekly, not just intentions?
- Do I review misses without excuses and adjust my system?

Learning and adaptation

- After setbacks, do I change inputs and constraints, not just "try harder"?
- Do I seek feedback and incorporate it into my routines?

Environment and friction

- Is my environment set up to make good choices easy and bad ones hard?
- Do I prepare tools and materials ahead of time to lower activation energy?

Under pressure

- When I'm stressed or busy, do my core habits hold?
- Can I say "No" to protect priorities without guilt or overexplaining?

Integrity between plans and actions

- If someone watched my day, would they see my calendar reflected in my actions?
- Do I choose important over urgent when they conflict?

CHAPTER 5

★★★★★★★

Humility

I enjoy watching a good magic show. The anticipation of how I will be amazed brings out a "kid-like" quality in me. Whether it's a routine illusion or the grand finale, I can be mesmerized by the elements of the presentation. Christopher Priest describes those components like this, "Every great magic trick consists of three parts or acts. The first part is called "The Pledge." The magician shows you something ordinary: a deck of cards, a bird, or a man. He shows you this object. Perhaps he asks you to inspect it to see if it is indeed real, unaltered, normal. But of course, it probably isn't. The second act is called "The Turn." The magician takes the ordinary something and makes it do something extraordinary. Now you're looking for the secret . . . but you won't find it, because, of course, you're not really looking. You don't really want to know. You want to be fooled. But you wouldn't clap yet. Because making something disappear isn't enough; you have to bring it back. That's why every magic trick has a third act, the hardest part, the part we call "The Prestige."

Due to skill, practice, and my preconceived ideas, the magician uses the pledge, turn, and prestige to either make me not see something that is there or see something that's not there. Remarkable.

Perhaps, there is some science behind the magic. "Selective Attention" is the process of focusing on a particular object in the environment for a certain period of time. Attention is a limited resource, so Selective Attention allows us to tune out unimportant details and focus on what really matters. In the magic trick, the magician enhances the trick's likelihood of success, because he defines or highlights the important details. He minimizes the unimportant parts, thus causing our Selective Attention to be honed as he prefers.

Selective Attention even affects us when it comes to seeing people. We can completely miss a person. "In order to sustain our attention to one event in everyday life, we must filter out other events," explains author Russell Revlin in his text *Cognition: Theory and Practice.* "We must be selective in our attention by focusing on some events to the detriment of others. This is because attention is like a resource that needs to be distributed to those events that are important." Since attention is a limited resource, we make conscious and unconscious judgments to determine importance and priority. Therefore, we make those same assessments when it comes to people. We see some people as relevant or important in a certain circumstance and others as inconsequential.

This exercise of force-ranking, or racking and stacking people, plays out daily in the numerous meetings we attend. Are there assigned seats in the meetings you attend? Maybe seats are not designated, but are there assessments or judgments made about the importance of roles? Is there a stated or unstated understanding as to the value of individuals in attendance? Who is the most important person in the room? Is it the boss or the person who controls the money? Is it the person with the best idea? Maybe it's the person with the right answer. What about the person who made the coffee or brought the doughnuts? What about the person who cleaned or set up the room before all of the invited participants arrived? What about the technology person who installed the Wi-Fi or connected the Apple TV?

Any of those could be the right answer, and I've been in plenty of meetings where they are conducted as such. As I have been called on to lead, the only thing I can definitively say on the subject is that I am never the most important person in the room. I know only what I know. I'm only a product of my experiences. I'm only so self-aware. Everyone else in the room brings a treasure trove of life that I have not been privy to. Inside these experiences are key questions and answers that will provide valuable insight to furthering the vision of our gathering.

With its tradition, rank structure, formal nature, and overabundance of type-A people, the military would appear to be the last place to find an environment where value is seen in everyone. However, you learn fairly quickly that everyone in your flight, squad, or unit is needed—and, therefore, valuable. The Air Force's Officer Training School (OTS) is divided into four phases of development. In Phase One, the goal is to "focus on teamwork, discipline, and standardization." Additionally, candidates will "acquire the skills needed to form and operate as a team as you begin to learn the fundamentals of leadership . . ." The Air Force's core values—*Integrity First, Service Before Self, Excellence in All We Do*—are rooted in both personal expectations and team accountability. Each phase of training at OTS has a series of samples of behaviors (known as SOBs) that highlight the building blocks of the major areas of learning. For example, learning teamwork is the overarching concept. The officer candidates are exposed to and expected to master specific skills, like sharing the load while working together, valuing diverse options, and embracing varied experiences and knowledge. These characteristics may be reinforced by conducting an exercise like carrying a giant log through challenging terrain to help trainees experience the need for everyone on the team to contribute. Or, you may be required to navigate an obstacle course where the completion of every member accounts for the unit's score rather than a single individual's effort.

The Leadership Reaction Course (LRC) is one of the capstone events of Officer Training School. The LRC is a series of approximately a dozen stations. Each station consists of a different obstacle and problem. The unit is charged with successfully completing the obstacle in the time constraints provided. The instructions for the LRC include the following statements:

Purpose and Objective of LRC

- Provides a method to observe and apply the applications of:
    - Leadership traits
    - Problem solving in a time-pressure situation
    - Management functions and principles
- Intent is to successfully apply the lessons taught in the flight room
- Your mission today: Successfully apply leadership-studies concepts to accomplish tasks
- All tasks require teamwork
- All team members must complete the task to be successful

Every person on the team matters, and success is measured by team effectiveness. Flying a mission from Ramstein Air Base, Germany, to Bagram Air Base, Afghanistan, takes not only the pilot, but maintenance personnel, services to fuel the jet, weather forecasters, intelligence officers, air-traffic controllers, not to mention the medical personnel and administrative team that cares for every member who has a part in this mission. Teamwork makes the dream work.

In order to further expand on this idea that every team member matters and that it takes humility to see them, below are a few examples of people you might have missed or dismissed if you were not humble enough to look for potential.

Leslie Lynch King, Jr., was born on July 14, 1913. His father, Leslie King, Sr., was an alcoholic and abusive to his wife, Dorothy Gardner. Only sixteen days after Leslie Jr.'s birth, the couple separated. The separation was sparked by an incident in which King, Sr. took a butcher knife and threatened to kill his wife, young son, and a nursemaid. The next few years were difficult for a single mother and a young son. They bounced around, living with various relatives for a while.

They eventually settled in Grand Rapids, Michigan. While there, Gardner met and married a nice man who worked in a family-owned paint and varnish store. Young Leslie was a hard worker and displayed gifts both academically and athletically. He attended the University of Michigan and majored in Economics. He played football and was a part of two national-championship teams. Following graduation, he applied to Yale Law School but was rejected. He made application again a couple of years later and was accepted. He finished third in his graduation class from Yale in 1941.

Later that year, after the Japanese attacked Pearl Harbor, King joined the Navy. He served four years, with significant combat action in the Pacific theater. Following the war, he entered politics. He won election to the U.S. House of Representatives in 1948 and served for twenty-five years. He was elected Vice President of the United States in 1972 and became President in 1974. You might recognize him by the name he took from his stepfather in 1935, Gerald R. Ford. It takes humility to see a future president in the face of a child whose father abandoned him a little more than two weeks after his birth.

Michael was born in Atlanta, Georgia, in 1929. He was the eldest child of a pastor. A gifted student, Michael entered college at the age of fifteen after skipping grades nine through twelve. He was Doogie Howser before Neil Patrick Harris was. After finishing his undergraduate work, he received a divinity degree and, then, a PhD from the prestigious Boston University in 1955. Somewhere among all of the promise, something must have gone wrong. Over the next dozen years, Michael was arrested twenty-nine times.

Clearly, a résumé like this would make any reasonable person judge the character of this man. He's not worth my investment, my attention, or my support since he displays such a lack of discipline. His arrest record includes violations such as driving thirty mph in a twenty-five mph zone. He was incarcerated for holding a prayer vigil. He was arrested for sitting at the wrong counter in a restaurant. He was jailed for protesting illegal voting restrictions. He was arrested for being on a sidewalk and parading without a permit.

This incorrigible young man was originally born Michael, but his father changed his name when he was five years old to Martin. Pride, arrogance, and assumption would have you miss this preacher's son who could not stop his criminal activity. Trapped in that blind spot, you would miss a man who once said he hoped for a world where people would not be "judged by the color of their skin but by the content of their character." Looking through the lens of humility would help you see Martin Luther King, who lived and died to see a dream come true.

Thomas was the kid nobody knew. Nobody knew him, because he was always the new kid. By the time he was 10 years old, he had lived in 10 different houses. His parents were divorced, and Thomas lived with his Dad and two of his siblings. Moving and adolescent awkwardness contributed to Thomas being painfully shy. In an attempt to overcome these obstacles, he tried to make people laugh. He was mildly successful. This led to his interest in acting and theater, which he participated in during high school. We all know that guy. He's not the athlete. He's not the heart-throb. He's a bit annoying and becomes overly obsessive as soon as he finds his niche. He studied theater in college. What other prospects did he have? He acted in some plays but wasn't really making it. He moved to New York, and the same track record followed him. He lowered his standards and accepted a role in a television series. This produced other opportunities, and Thomas just kept showing up for work. His diversity was his trademark. He played an astronaut and an attorney. He was the voice of a toy and he toyed with a volcano. You might have missed a Hollywood icon if you had ignored the perpetual new kid in class named Tom Hanks.

Author Jim Collins said, "The difference between a good leader and a great leader is humility." He went on to say, "Level-Five leaders are differentiated from other levels of leaders in that they have a wonderful blend of personal humility combined with extraordinary professional will. Understand that they are very ambitious; but their ambition, first and foremost, is for the company's success. They realize that the most important step they must make to become a Level-Five leader is to subjugate their ego to the company's performance. When asked for interviews, these leaders will agree only if it's about the company and not about them."

Jim Moschgat learned this lesson while a cadet at the United States Air Force Academy. Jim and the other four thousand cadets were the future leaders of the Air Force. Their daily activities included academics, athletics, and military training. Like other college students, they lived in dormitories. While the facilities were kept more in order than an average dormitory, it still required someone to attend to the details. William "Bill" Crawford was that someone. As the janitor, his duties included mopping and buffing floors, emptying trash cans, cleaning toilets, or just tidying up the mess of roughly one hundred college kids.

Few people noticed Bill. Occasionally, he received a passing greeting but, at other times, no acknowledgment at all. He always kept the building spotlessly clean—even the toilets and showers gleamed. Frankly, he did his job so well, no one noticed or got involved. After all, cleaning toilets was his job. Bill didn't move very quickly and, in fact, you could even say that he shuffled a bit, as if he suffered from some sort of injury. His gray hair and wrinkled face made him appear ancient to a group of young cadets. And his crooked smile, well, it looked a little funny. Face it, Bill was an old man working in a young person's world. What did he have to offer?

His personality rendered him almost invisible to the young people around him. Bill was shy, almost painfully so. He seldom spoke to a cadet unless they addressed him first, and that didn't happen very often. He buried himself in his work, moving about with stooped shoulders, a quiet gait, and an averted gaze. If he noticed the hustle and bustle of cadet life around him, it was hard to tell. Bill blended into the woodwork and became just another fixture around the building. The Academy, one of our nation's premier leadership laboratories, kept its residents busy from dawn till dusk. And Mr. Crawford, well, he was just a janitor.

All that changed for Jim Moschgat after reading a book about World War II and the Allied ground campaign in Italy. He read an incredible story that said that on Sept. 13, 1943, a Private William Crawford from Colorado, assigned to the 36th Infantry Division, had been involved in some bloody fighting on Hill 424 near Altavilla, Italy. "In the face of intense and overwhelming hostile fire . . . with no regard for personal safety . . . on his own initiative, Private Crawford single-handedly attacked fortified enemy positions." It continued, "for conspicuous gallantry and intrepidity at risk of life above and beyond the call of duty, the President of the United States awards the Medal of Honor to Private William Crawford."

William Crawford, the janitor, had received the highest and most prestigious personal military decoration that can be awarded to a U.S. serviceman. If you took the entire cadet corps and seated them in the Holaday Athletic Center, not one of them would receive the honor and military courtesies that Bill had. He might be considered the most important person in the room.

Based on his experience with William "Bill" Crawford, Jim Moschgat penned "A Janitor's Ten Lessons in Leadership." These thoughts can also help you see the value of everyone in the room.

1. Be cautious of labels. Labels you place on people may define your relationship to them and bind their potential. Be cautious of a leader who flippantly says, "Hey, he's just a ____." That person might just save your life one day.

2. Everyone deserves respect. Respect should not be reserved for only those with lofty titles. Respect is a basic human principle. Mr. Crawford deserved respect because he was a janitor, walked among them, and was a part of their team.

3. Courtesy makes a difference. Be courteous to all around you, regardless of title or position. Common courtesies help bond a team.

4. Take time to know your people. Life is hectic, but that's no excuse for not knowing the people who work for and with you.

5. Anyone can be a hero. Don't sell your people short, for any one of them may be the hero who rises to the occasion when duty calls.

6. Leaders should be humble. Most modern-day heroes and some leaders are anything but humble. Not Mr. Crawford—he was too busy working to celebrate his past heroics. Leaders would be well-served to do the same.

7. Life won't always hand you what you think you deserve. You may not get the recognition you feel you deserve, but sometimes you just have to persevere. Perhaps you weren't nominated for an award or promotion you thought you should get. Don't let that stop you.

8. Don't pursue glory; pursue excellence. Private Crawford didn't pursue glory; he did his duty and then swept floors for a living. No matter what task life hands you, do it well.

9. No job is beneath a leader. If Mr. Crawford, a Medal of Honor winner, could clean latrines and smile, is there a job beneath your dignity?

10. Life is a leadership laboratory. All too often, we look to some school or professional-education class to teach us about leadership when, in fact, life is a leadership laboratory. Those you meet every day will teach you enduring lessons if you just take time to stop, look, and listen.

Leaders are humble. Jesus washed the feet of his twelve disciples (John 13:1–17). He said he did that as an example to them. His example is extraordinary. He showed service to others; he displayed that no task is beneath the leader. He washed the feet of a man he knew would betray him. Anyone can be humble toward those who can return the favor or even reward you for your actions. The humble person acts when the reward might be a knife in the back or a treasonous kiss on the cheek. Leaders don't look around for who can do something; they do it in humility.

Application

The self-audit below helps identify areas of humility versus pride. Pick three to five questions that sting, and journal one paragraph each. Choose one behavior to practice this week: ask one more question before speaking, acknowledge someone else publicly, or change one decision based on feedback. Revisit monthly, and note specific examples where you shifted from pride to humility in action.

Motives and posture

- Am I aiming to serve the goal and people involved, or to be seen as right or impressive?
- If no one knew I did this, would I still make the same choice?
- Do I enter conversations curious to learn—or prepared to win?

Listening and learning

- Did I ask clarifying questions before offering my view?
- Can I state the strongest version of others' perspectives fairly?
- What did I change my mind about based on new information?

Credit and blame

- Do I share credit quickly and specifically?
- When things go well, do I spotlight the team's contributions more than my own?
- When things go poorly, do I own my part without excuses?

Feedback and correction

- Do I invite candid feedback from people who might disagree with me?
- When corrected, do I thank the person and adjust my behavior promptly?
- What feedback have I acted on in the past month?

Status and deference

- Do I treat those with less power or visibility with the same respect as I treat those with more?
- Do I make space for quieter voices and adjust the pace so others can contribute?
- Have I reversed a decision because someone else's idea was better?

Confidence vs. arrogance

- Am I clear about what I know, what I don't, and where I'm guessing?
- Do I hold strong opinions lightly enough to update them?
- Does my confidence rest on evidence and preparation, not on entitlement?

Language and tone

- Are my words plain, honest, and respectful, or inflated and self-centering?
- Do I interrupt, dominate airtime, or use "I/me" far more than "we/you"?
- Would a neutral observer describe my tone as open or defensive?

Service and sacrifice

- What cost am I willing to bear for the sake of the mission or others?
- Do I take on unglamorous tasks when they are the right thing to do?
- Am I mentoring or developing others, not just advancing myself?

Perspective and gratitude

- What am I grateful for that I did not earn alone?
- Who helped me get here, and have I thanked them recently?
- Do I regularly acknowledge limits and dependence on others?

Signs of pride creep

- Am I irritated by being overlooked, questioned, or slowed down?
- Do I quietly keep score of recognition or comparison with peers?
- Have I avoided an apology I owe?

CHAPTER 6

★★★★★★★

Courage

I can't think of a word that carries more weight in my mind, body, and spirit than "courage." Courage is a core characteristic and value. It's also personified in countless situations I've observed and stories I've heard. The earliest records of the word "courage" come from Old French "*corage*" or "*cuer*" meaning "heart." So, courage might be displayed in action, but it originates in the heart.

Elizabeth Busching is a counselor. She says that often the highest values in your family are never spoken or written. They are simply understood. Courage is a Wiggins family value. Leo and Iris Wiggins never *told* me to be courageous. They *modeled* the quality, and because you were a part of their tribe, it was expected that you would live it, just like any other DNA attribute that coursed through your body.

I was born in 1962 in Huntsville, Alabama. Our family relocated to East Point, Georgia, a suburb of Atlanta, in 1966. For the next ten years, we resided in a middle-class neighborhood near Georgia's state capitol. "Middle class" is an interesting term. I had always heard it but was unsure what it actually meant. With several years of experience behind me, I believe what it implied was middle-class white. I don't remember many kids in my school who didn't look like me. I don't remember many kids at church who didn't look like me. I don't remember many kids in my athletic leagues who didn't look like me. I know there are boatloads of books as to the why, what, and how of that experience, but that isn't this book. I was a kid growing up going to school, church, and the playgrounds, and it was on a playground that I saw courage come to life.

I was playing for the East Point Tigers in recreational-league football. My dad was one of the assistant coaches. We showed up for one of our games, and I saw a commotion. One of the kids on the other team was crying. He was being consoled by his mom. As I looked a few yards away from him, there was a man holding a stick that had a rope attached to it. At the end of the rope was a football jersey and football pants stuffed with something. The jersey was the same color as the opposing team, and the number was the same number as the kid crying. The kid was black. The man holding the stick was white. The man was shouting words that I didn't understand. My dad said, "Wait here, Scottie Boy." I obeyed.

In the deep South in the late 1960s and early 1970s, there were generally three kinds of people, from my eight-year-old perspective. There were people who were racist by word and deed. There were people who were racist by a lack of word or deed. Then, there were people who fought against hate, any kind of hate. Leo Wiggins didn't tolerate hate.

My dad was not a violent man. In fact, my dad was loving, kind, generous, and compassionate. But, my Korean-War veteran dad was also a man of conviction and courage. He opened up a can of courage on the man with the stick. Stick man left the field. Unfortunately, so did the little boy on the other team. I can't imagine how hurt, sad, and traumatized he was. Courage stands against hate.

Courage doesn't have a nationality, ethnicity, height, weight, or gender requirement. Natalia Dmytruk is proof that it comes wrapped in all forms. The 2022 Russian aggression against Ukraine is just the latest in a long line of conflict between Russia and Ukraine. The 2004 Ukrainian Presidential Election is another example. The Ukrainian candidate, Viktor Yushchenko, appeared to be a clear favorite, defeating the Russian-backed candidate Viktor Yanukovych for the presidency. During the state-run television evening-news telecast, the announcers declared the Russian-backed candidate the winner as the script indicated. Everyone knew it was a lie, but they were afraid to speak up—everyone but Natalia. Natalia was the deaf language interpreter on the broadcast. None of the government or military officials understood sign language. She chose to sign the truth. She signed "Our president is Viktor Yushchenko. Do not trust the results of the central election committee. They are all lies." This act served as a catalyst that birthed the Orange Revolution in Ukraine, demanding election reform. This prompted the nation's Supreme Court to review the election, ultimately declaring Yushchenko the winner. One would assume that, in the aftermath, there would be a "Natalia Dmytruk Day," and she would be lauded and loved by her employers. The state-run television showed their appreciation by eliminating sign-language services from their broadcasts. She was recognized with awards for bravery and freedom from other nations. Jesus once said a prophet doesn't receive any honor in his hometown. Natalia wasn't seeking honor, but what she did display was courage that stands up for truth.

U.S Army Captain William Swenson was just doing his job on September 8, 2009. He was protecting a convoy of vehicles full of Afghan leaders who were going to attend a tribal summit of elders. The vehicle caravan was going through a dangerous part of northern Afghanistan when the Taliban attacked. The group was attacked on nearly every side. About an hour into the firefight, Sgt. First Class Kenneth Westbrook, in an exposed position, yelled to Swenson that he'd been hit. Westbrook was Swenson's right-hand man. Despite his injuries, Westbrook kept fighting. Eventually, he started to fade from his wounds, and yelled, "I can't keep this up," which prompted Swenson to expose himself to the hostile fire to tend to him. Westbrook mustered what Swenson said was incredible strength and determination to move hundreds of yards, bobbing up and down to avoid getting hit again as he headed for an evacuation helicopter. Swenson said he offered support, as well as covering fire. In a brief moment captured on a camera mounted on the helmet of one of the pilots on the air-evac helicopter, he placed a kiss on Westbrook's forehead before leaving him. When asked why, Swenson responded, "A simple act of compassion and loyalty to a brother-in-arms. I was just trying to keep his spirits up. I wanted him to know it was going to be OK."

This battle raged for more than six hours. Swenson was awarded the Medal of Honor for his actions. He displayed great physical courage that day, yet his greatest act of courage was showing someone that he loved them.

Then, there's Ken Reinhardt. Ken was a high-school student in Little Rock, Arkansas. He saw the gross injustice that was racism. When nine African-American students showed up to go to his all-white school, Ken saw that most people opposed their admission. The students faced physical and verbal abuse. Ken observed this atrocious behavior and wanted to do something. Ken didn't wave a gun, he didn't make a speech, he didn't get on Instagram and post a picture, or release something on Tik Tok. He didn't talk about doing something; Ken *did* something. Ken offered to walk with the students to class. Ken offered to be a friend when these students didn't have any friends. Sometimes courage is simply being a friend.

Courage is on speed dial in every environment we occupy. It might be required at school, work, home, and all places in between. While the locations are vast, courage originates from three distinct places. 1 Thessalonians 5:23 identifies them: "Now may the God of peace himself sanctify you completely, and may your whole spirit and soul and body be kept blameless at the coming of our Lord Jesus Christ." The Bible says we have a body, soul, and spirit. The body is our physical nature—its arms, legs, torso, internal organs, central nervous system, and more. It's the cumulative things that make you a physical organism. The soul is your inner life. It's your mind, will, emotions, memories, imagination, personality, and relationships. It's all the non-physical things that make you, well, *you*. The spirit is what comes to life when a person accepts the work of Jesus personally. It's the act of 1 Corinthians 5:17, which proclaims you are a "new creation." The spirit was dead, but with Christ, it is made alive according to Ephesians 2:4–5. Since we have these three distinct aspects—body, soul, and spirit—courage is exercised in each uniquely.

Courage of the Body (Physical)

Physical courage is commonly the thing that comes to mind when most people think about courage. Perhaps it is the only type of courage you are even aware of! So, what is physical courage? It is the ability to face danger, pain, and fear. It's seen in people who have received injuries while trying to save someone else or those who have been through trauma that has left them with lasting physical scars. Air Force TSgt. John Chapman and SrA Jason Cunningham exhibited this type of character in March 2002 at the Battle of Takur Ghar in Afghanistan.

Military members might get more opportunities to display physical courage, but they don't have a monopoly on it. John Sampson jumped on the monorail track at Hersheypark in 2025 to rescue a child who had wandered onto the track. Wendal Tucker ran into oncoming traffic to usher a six-year-old girl to safety. Buffalo, New York, resident Sarah Brown happened upon an automobile accident where the driver was unresponsive. She performed CPR, reviving the man and saving his life. Physical courage can also be seen in people who face their fears, like skydivers or firefighters, despite the possibility of getting hurt.

While this type of courage may seem like it requires physical strength, sometimes it just requires mental and emotional strength. Physical courage is more than risking life and limb. It's putting yourself in harm's way for someone else. Facing a situation threatening the safety or life of another requires physical courage. It's making your legs and arms move in one direction when your central nervous system is sending messages to your appendages saying, "Flight or freeze." It's taking a step or issuing a warning without thought to the potential consequences of these actions.

Courage of the Soul

Sometimes courage is called upon by your mind, your emotions, or a set of values you've adopted. Courage of the soul allows you to face your fears and overcome them, no matter how terrifying they may be. Choosing calm over an angry outburst, walking away rather than engaging the hysterics, extending grace rather than holding a grudge, admitting you don't have the answer, owning your part of a conflict even when the other person fails to admit their portion, and ending a professional or personal relationship are all aspects of this type of bravery.

Other monikers for this type of courage are social, ethical, moral, or personal. Regardless of the branding, courage of the soul is displayed when you speak up in meetings even when you have no allies. It shows up when you challenge management, share opinions that aren't popular, or point out a flaw in a plan. Sometimes this type of courage makes decisions based on what makes sense intellectually rather than what's easiest or most comfortable.

"You can be strong as a leader and be kind.
You can be courageous as a leader and be fearful.
You can be a leader without the title.
But first comes courage."
—Sonia McDonald

When a situation calls you to risk embarrassment, rejection, image, or status, you're exercising courage of the soul. It can look like presenting an opposing view in a meeting when leadership appears to be aligned on the opposite side. U.S. Army General David McKiernan, who led all NATO and US troops in Afghanistan in 2009, was relieved of command by expressing opposition to U.S. strategy in the region in private and appropriate settings. He chose courage of the soul over comfort and going along. It takes this kind of fortitude to stand up for yourself. If someone constantly interrupts you, talks over you, or dismisses you because "you're just the administrative assistant," you exercise this kind of bravery. By making this stand, you give voice to others who experience the same prejudice but have not advanced in using their social-courage muscles. Sometimes social courage is admitting a mistake with honesty and without excuse. Acknowledging that you should have acted on someone's advice or confessing that you were impatient or fearful are honest ways to recognize and recover from mistakes.

William Slim, a former Governor-General of Australia, said, "Moral courage is a higher and a rarer virtue than physical courage." Moral courage or courage of the soul is required when your ethics, your code, or your ethos is challenged. Embarrassment, loss of status, and judgment by others is a risk factor when exercising soul courage, but there are even greater consequences. Compromising your ethics is like exposing your soul to a virus. A single exposure might not be deadly, but it reduces your ability to ward off future attacks. Eventually, your moral code is so eroded that you are standing on a foundation of quicksand.

Seneca said, "No advantage can be of use if it costs you your honor." Marcus Aurelius added, "If it is not right, do not do it; if it is not true, do not say it."

Soul courage cannot be a line in the sand. It must be an impenetrable forcefield, a no-fly zone, an unquestionable commitment to an ideal greater than yourself. Calling out financial impropriety, confronting immoral behavior, and reporting breaks in policy and law are hard—but right. Additionally, rationalization is the grease used to coat the downward slope of ethical concession. "It will not happen again," or "Just this once," or "For this person or position, it's OK," or "This circumstance is unique," are all attacks on the armor of morality. Face these threats with overwhelming resolve and complete, uncompromising commitment. This shall not pass.

Courage of the Spirit

Spiritual courage is the willingness to live a counter-cultural life and make difficult choices. It's a willingness to risk what you think you know to learn more about yourself. This type of courage is essential if you want to overcome personal fears, limiting beliefs, and a very real spiritual enemy. It's determining to let truth and love rule your actions. It is unconcerned with outward appearances and completely devoted to being light to a dark world. There is no shortage of references to the truth that spiritual courage is required and will be tested. John 16:33 says we will face trials. John 10:10 says our enemy is out to annihilate us. 1 Peter 5:8 says our enemy wants to consume us. In response to this force, Paul uses the admonition "Be strong" to his apprentice, Timothy, twenty-five times.

The action phase of being strong is many times spurred on by a quiet voice or an almost-imperceptible nudge in your soul. It can be an ache, a gnawing inside that is perpendicular to your spiritual character. It takes this kind of mettle to tell the senior leadership of a church that their actions prove they value a slick performance in Sunday-morning church rather than worship. Spiritual courage is required to confront prejudicial behavior toward a person's gender or ethnicity. Isaiah provided the perfect response when faced with this type of challenge. He said in Isaiah 6:8, "Here I am. Send me."

Courageous people are often called "heroes" because they do what others would not dare to do—even at significant personal risk. But what makes someone courageous? Courage is about facing your fears, pain, or danger. Courage is being scared of something but doing it anyway.

It's hard to personally reflect and cite instances of courage—isn't *humility* one of the aspects of courage? Self-reflection and boasting are a form of thin ice—you must walk gingerly to find proof of where your heart and actions aligned to signify this quality in yourself. In First Corinthians 15:9, the apostle Paul writes that he is the least of all of the apostles, that he isn't worthy to be categorized as such. Similarly, I'm unworthy to stand alongside the men and women mentioned in this chapter. I can only cite a singular occurrence that warrants mentioning.

It was August 20, 2021 at 10:28 a.m. It was a hot Mississippi summer morning. I'd just finished cutting my grass. My clothes were drenched with sweat. I was mildly physically tired, but that didn't scratch the surface of my overall wellness. I was mentally exhausted and emotionally empty. Following twenty-eight years of military service and eight years of ministry in the local church, I had reached my limit. For years, Jennabeth and I had discussed my need to seek mental and emotional help from a counselor. My wife supported and suggested but didn't demand or nag. I addressed the problem with passivity, assuming that, if it got bad enough, Jennabeth would step in and insist. Something happened inside of me on this day that I couldn't explain, but my mind, body, and soul were looking at the record of my past—and they were finding that payment was required. I did the most courageous thing I could do. I called for help.

I made a call to Elizabeth Busching. Elizabeth is a ministry friend I'd met years earlier. She is a counselor by education, training, and practice, and a trusted advisor and confidante. Over the years, I had contacted Elizabeth to refer people to her, but on August 21, 2021, I made a different request. "I'm calling for me," I said. I didn't have the stamina or pride to pretend anymore. I was dying on the inside, and I was figuratively crawling for water for my parched soul. I met with Elizabeth on September 3, and she agreed to work with me. This began my prioritization and pursuit of my total health. Courage means you're vulnerable enough to ask for and accept help.

Billy is a person who knows about courage. Author and pastor Tony Campolo told me how he had been asked years ago to be a counselor at a junior-high summer Bible camp. He observed that a junior-high kid's concept of a good time is picking on other kids. And at this particular camp, there was a little boy named Billy, who was suffering from cerebral palsy. As Billy walked across the camp with his uncoordinated body, the other kids would line up and imitate his strange movements, teasing him mercilessly. One day, Billy was asking for directions. "Which way is the craft shop?" he stammered, his mouth contorting. And the boys mimicked him in that same mocking, stuttering, "It's over . . . there . . . Billy." And then they laughed at him.

Two days later, it was Billy's cabin's turn to give morning devotions and prayers. Tony wondered what would happen, because his fellow cabin mates had appointed Billy to be the speaker. Tony knew that they just wanted to get Billy up there to make fun of him. As Billy dragged his body to the front, you could hear the giggles rolling over the crowd. It took him almost five minutes to say seven words. The young boy's stammering words fell from his mouth with no grace or eloquence. "Jesus . . . loves . . . me . . . , and . . . I . . . love . . . Jesus!" When Billy finished, there was dead silence. Tony looked over his shoulder and saw junior-high boys crying all over the place.

A revival broke out in that camp after Billy's short testimony. Tony says that, as he travels all over the world, he finds missionaries and pastors who say, "Remember me? I was converted at that junior-high summer Bible camp." The counselor had tried everything to get those kids interested in Jesus, even bringing in well-known baseball players whose batting averages had gone up since they had started praying. But God didn't use the superstars. God chose to use a kid with cerebral palsy. Matthew 6:33 and 11:28 are often paraphrased into, "If you take the first step, God will take the rest." Despite what the world would label as challenges and handicaps, Billy took the first step, and look what God did through him with the rest.

Courage is selfless.
Courage is humble.
Courage is kind.
Courage is thorough, long-suffering, and resilient.
Courage is steadfast; it stays.
Courage is love.
Courage stands against hate.
Courage is being vulnerable enough to say, "I need help."

Some people prefer comfort over courage, clinging to the known room with the worn-out chair instead of stepping into the hallway, where the light is new. They call it "peace," but it's often a hush that hides a shrinking horizon, a lullaby that keeps their boldness asleep. Courage asks, "What if I try?" while comfort whispers, "What if I fail?" And so, days pass, tidy and tame, until the life they wanted is only a rumor, and the life they lived is a careful circle with no doors. George Eliot said, "It's never too late to be what you might have been." Choose courage, and lead the church likewise.

Application

Review the questions below. Answer, using a specific moment from the last thirty to sixty days. Write one sentence for each section below. Commit to one courageous micro-step in the next hour, and calendar it. Review afterward: What did I learn, and what rule will I carry forward?

Intent and values

- Am I acting to serve a meaningful value or mission, not ego or impulse?
- If I do nothing, what important value gets compromised?

Risk and cost

- What am I afraid of right now, specifically?
- What is the real (not imagined) worst-case scenario, and can I survive or mitigate it?
- What is the cost of delay vs. the cost of imperfect action?

Truth and candor

- Am I willing to say the needed hard thing clearly and respectfully?
- Have I named the elephant in the room to the right people?

Responsibility and stakes

- Who benefits if I act, and who bears the risk?
- Do I have the authority or duty to step in, and what does that require?

Choice of action

- What is the smallest bold step that advances the goal and buys information?
- Is the step reversible if new facts emerge?

Integrity under pressure

- Am I choosing the principled path, even if it is unpopular or costly?
- Would I take the same action if no one ever knew?

Resilience and recovery

- If this fails, what is my recovery plan?
- What support or ally can I engage to strengthen my stance?

Learning signal

- What will I learn by acting that I can't learn by waiting?
- What evidence would make me pivot or double down?

Body and emotion check

- Is my hesitation coming from fear of discomfort or from a real safety signal?
- After a deep breath, does the action still align with my values?

CHAPTER 7

★★★★★★★

Intelligence, Surveillance, Reconnaissance (ISR)

It was September 2004. I was flying a mission from Incirlik Air Base, Turkey, to Tikrit, Iraq (also known as Contingency Operating Base [COB] Speicher), followed by a short hop to Kirkuk, Iraq, commonly referred to as K1 Air Base. I'd flown this route many times. It traverses Northern Iraq and crosses into an area known as the Sunni Triangle. So called because of the dense population of Sunni Muslims, it is an area where some intense fighting has occurred in places like Ramadi and Fallujah. Prior to arriving at the airplane, my first stop was C2—Command and Control—to receive a mission brief.

The mission brief has several elements. You're briefed on the primary objective, sequence of events, participating forces, and notices to airmen (NOTAMS), which are aviation alerts. Additionally, you receive an update on the maintenance status of the airplane, the expected route of flight, and weather. With this information in hand, you proceed to a Sensitive Compartmented Information Facility (SCIF) to receive an intelligence briefing.

The intelligence briefing provides the pilot information on threats, targets, situational awareness regarding concurrent military operations, and escape-and-evasion plans, should this become necessary. The briefing also provides cultural information—local and national politics, economic issues, and societal practices. At that point, three years after 9/11, I'd received literally hundreds of intelligence briefings. Having flown this route and mission previously, I'd been updated on this exact information several times. Regardless of the redundancy, I listened this time as if I had never heard the briefing before.

Intelligence and two of its key components—surveillance and reconnaissance—matter to leaders. It allows a leader to see before acting. Leaders make decisions in uncertainty. Intelligence, Surveillance, and Reconnaissance (ISR) reduce that uncertainty, so that choices are faster, wiser, and more resilient. Whether you are flying a jet, leading a platoon, in charge of a section at your job, or part of a church, ISR is the disciplined practice of answering three questions continuously: What is happening? What might happen next? What should we do about it?

A working definition of our core concepts is important.

- Intelligence: Processed information that answers decision-making needs. Intelligence is not data; it is data interpreted in context to reduce uncertainty for a specific decision. Intelligence takes surveillance and reconnaissance, and turns both into insight tied to decisions.
- Surveillance: Systematic, ongoing monitoring of an area, domain, or set of indicators. Think of it as your "always-on sensors." Surveillance finds the baseline and detects deviations.
- Reconnaissance: Targeted, time-bound collection to fill specific knowledge gaps. Think of it as your "go look" missions. Reconnaissance investigates the deviation or answers a focused question.

It might be easy to dismiss ISR as a leadership quality. It's easy to see how characteristics like courage, humility, and commitment are important. But ISR? Did I just need another chapter in this book? How can a concept so rooted in military, clandestine, or law-enforcement environments have any relevance to leadership? Even if supported, how do you tie its applicability to leadership in the church? Why is ISR imperative to leadership? Here are five reasons.

1. Better timing: The quality of a decision is often a function of when it is made, not just what is decided. ISR gives earlier warning and more options.
2. Resource economy: You can't mass resources everywhere. ISR helps prioritize the decisive point and avoid waste.
3. Risk management: Many risks are visible only in weak signals. Surveillance detects signal drift; recon validates whether it matters.
4. Tempo advantage: ISR accelerates the Observe-Orient-Decide-Act (OODA) loop. Faster, more accurate orientation compounds advantage over time.
5. Trust and credibility: Leaders who consistently "see around corners" build confidence in teams, stakeholders, and partners.

While using a negative to prove a point isn't the most encouraging way to solidify your stance, it can serve as a cautionary tale when something like ISR is ignored.

Operation Anaconda was an early effort in the war on terrorism to deliver a blow to al-Qaeda and supporting Taliban forces in the Shahi-Kot-Valley of Afghanistan. In order to support troops engaged in the operation, a quick-reaction force (QRF), made up of USAF Special Tactics, Army Rangers, and Navy SEALs was inserted on

Takur Ghar, a mountain overlooking the battlefield. Things went horribly wrong from the moment the two MH-47 Chinook helicopters prepared to land. Enemy-troop strength was grossly underestimated. The weather and the presence of snow on the ground was inaccurately reported. Even when a subsequent rescue mission was dispatched, the follow-on intelligence was not relayed, and troops were wearing summer-weight clothing, as they were not briefed on their landing location. This lack of information made for arduous going in the mountain snow. Seven men were killed and twelve wounded during this part of the operation.

Were there other contributing factors that caused this to be the most-deadly engagement of Operation Anaconda? Yes. Would a better intelligence report have saved lives? Absolutely. Years after the battle, surveillance video captured by a drone recorded the heroic efforts of Air Force MSgt. John Chapman as he fought off a numerically superior force to protect his fellow special operators. Chapman was posthumously awarded the Medal of Honor for his actions. The drone footage is the only video record of a medal-of-honor recipient's actions. Tragically, an agency was monitoring that drone video feed in real time, but their information was never relayed to the forces on the ground or in the air. This was another missed opportunity for intelligence to effect a different outcome.

The 2012 movie *Zero Dark Thirty* is a work of historical fiction that offers a view of the Central Intelligence Agency's search for Osama Bin Laden. It does provide a glimpse into the painstakingly slow and methodical process of gathering intelligence. The glamor of a movie short-circuits the real-life laborious efforts required for fact-finding. The discipline involved in obtaining actionable intelligence is critical, because lives are at stake. The U.S.-backed invasion of Cuba in 1961, dubbed the "Bay of Pigs," was just such a failure. The CIA failed to provide President John Kennedy an assessment that the trained Cuban fighters could not succeed without direct U.S. military involvement. There were lapses prior to the attack on Pearl Harbor in 1941 and misses before the terrorist attacks on September 11, 2001. The 2023 Chinese spy balloons seemed to catch the federal government unprepared.

These accounts of ISR failures and lives lost may seem too sensational. What do actions like these have to do with leaders at the community church in your town or the First Denominational Church in a city near you? John 10:10 gives us insight into our enemy. Satan comes to "steal, kill, and destroy." So, his goal is total annihilation. With that in mind, your first step in intelligence gathering is simply believing the threat is real. Understanding capabilities and limitations is a vital aspect of gathering intelligence. Underestimating the enemy is a deadly mistake. In January 1968, North Vietnamese forces launched a massive assault on South Vietnam, called the Tet Offensive. While the advances were stayed, the surprise shocked the American people to such a degree that support for the war waned, leading to unrest, political division, and military confusion. Do not be naive. Satan observes your patterns and behaviors. He is crouching at your door (Genesis 4:7), so we are to be vigilant (1 Peter 5:8).

As Jesus was sending his disciples out in Matthew 10, He delivered a quintessential intelligence report. He named the members of the team (verses 2–4). He told them the route to take, how to go, and who to encounter (verses 5–6). He told them what to do along the way (verses 7–8). He covered logistics, human intelligence (HUMINT), and financial and cultural aspects of the journey (verses 9–15). Jesus reviewed threats and proper response when encountered by the enemy (verses 16–23). Jesus practiced and taught preparation as part of His process.

Author Warren Berger says, "By asking questions, we learn, analyze, and understand—and can move forward in the face of uncertainty.

When confronted with almost any demanding situation, in work or life, the act of questioning can help guide us to smart decisions and a sensible course of action." In Berger's book *The Book of Beautiful Questions*, he cites five enemies to asking questions. In order to defeat the enemy, you must identify him. The enemies are:

- Fear. Foremost among what I think of as the five enemies of questioning is fear. To ask a question is an admission that 1) You don't know and 2) you do care. Fear of asking questions can be particularly strong in the workplace. Employees worry, "Will asking questions make it seem as if I don't know how to do my job? Will it annoy my colleagues and supervisors, or, worse, will it threaten them in some way?" Often, in interviews, I'll ask candidates, "What are you pretending to know in your current job that you don't actually know?"
- Knowledge. The more you know, the less you feel you need to ask. First, we can easily fall into the "trap of expertise," wherein knowledgeable people begin to rely too much on what they already know and fail to keep expanding upon and updating their knowledge. In many of your meetings, people are looking to you for answers. Therefore, you are less likely to solicit their input through questioning. Why? Maybe the fear that we just discussed. Maybe time, which we'll discuss in a minute.
- Bias and Hubris. This brings up the third and fourth enemies of questioning, which are related to each other—bias and hubris. If we are predisposed to think something, we may be less open to considering questions that challenge that view. Self-questioning is an important characteristic. But to do that, we must also contend with hubris, which can lead us to believe our biases are correct or are not biases at all. Everybody else

is biased. The relationship between humility and questioning is interesting. If you lack the former, you'll probably do less of the latter.

- Time. The last enemy of questioning is time. Asking a question is often our last priority. We have to either download or receive information. George Carlin once said, "Some people see things that are and ask, 'Why?' Some people dream of things that never were and ask, 'Why not?' Some people have to go to work and don't have time for all that s***."

Building an ISR System

Parts of any ISR system include planning, collection, analysis, dissemination and feedback. Each of these five parts have equal value, but let me focus on planning. Planning a combat operation has unique challenges, and so does moving the world's most powerful leader. In 1996, I was hired by the Air Force's Special Air Mission division, based out of the Pentagon. As a pilot, I was assigned to Air Force One. Our mission was to provide air transportation for the president of the United States. Most people equate the Boeing 747 with the blue and white livery as Air Force One, but technically, any aircraft the president flies on is Air Force One.

The movement of the president takes an enormous team. The Air Force is only one part of an integrated force that includes the United States Marine Corps, the United States Secret Service (USSS), the Office of the White House, the White House Communications Agency (WHCA), and others. My role was to coordinate activities between Air Force One, the Executive Office of the President of the United States, the USSS, WHCA as referenced above, the Federal Aviation Administration (FAA), local law enforcement, and local airport authorities.

From the moment the president stepped onto Air Force One at Andrews AFB, Maryland, to the moment he stepped off the aircraft at a destination, until he disembarked safely back in Washington, the Air Force One team was responsible for the planning and execution of every detail of the trip. Each trip has its share of obstacles, and a flight from Andrews to Quonset Point, Rhode Island, followed by a short helicopter flight to Martha's Vineyard, requires just as much attention to detail as a seven-day South American trip that includes stops in Venezuela, Brazil, and Argentina. President Clinton's first trip to South America in October 1997 required masterful planning.

The diplomatic mission was really three trips in one, so the Brazil and Argentina components had similar planning requirements. Security is always a foremost concern, and the unpredictable political climate, specifically in Venezuela, was a pressing matter. Additionally, the overlapping agencies that required coordination made things more cumbersome. There are no clean lines between what local and national police are responsible for, and the military seizes control when they desire and without anyone's foreknowledge. The air-traffic system was fairly straightforward, and the support from the airport authority was excellent.

Sometimes the greatest challenges don't come from a foreign military or political power but from internal wrangling. Since this was President Clinton's first trip to these countries in his five years in office, the list of people vying for a seat on Air Force One was robust. The first lady and her staff were onboard, as were Secretary of State Madeline Albright; U.N. Ambassador Bill Richardson; Mack McLarty, the president's envoy to the region; Commerce Secretary Richard Daley; National Security Advisor Sandy Berger; Energy Secretary Federico Pena and drug czar Barry McCaffrey, along with their staffs. The congressional delegation included Connecticut Democratic Sen. Chris Dodd and Democratic Reps. Jim McDermott (Washington),

Nydia Velazquez (New York), and Ruben Hinojosa (Texas). Several members of the media rounded out a large contingent.

In addition to the number of people on the aircraft, ground operations at Simon Bolivar International Airport in Caracas were made difficult by local authorities as well as the White House. A Boeing 747 is a large airplane, but it's not the only plane associated with the trip. There was a separate commercial airline for additional members of the press corps. There were several other military aircraft to support the visit carrying WHCA personnel and equipment, USSS personnel, as well as presidential limos and motorcade support vehicles. Trying to find ramp space to park all of these airplanes and ensure their security twenty-four hours a day was a giant puzzle. Even after the plan was made, the First Lady wanted changes. She was particularly sensitive about the president coming down the stairs of Air Force One with U.S. military aircraft in the background of camera shots. All parking locations and security requirements had to be modified in meet this demand. Just because you have the responsibility of planning doesn't mean you have the final say-so on the plan. As we would say in the Air Force, flexibility is the key to air power. It's key in planning as well.

If you prefer a quote rather than a story, here are some to ponder.

"Give me six hours to chop down a tree,
and I'll spend the first four sharpening the axe."
—Abraham Lincoln

"For tomorrow belongs to the people who prepare for it today."
—African Proverb

"By failing to prepare, you are preparing to fail."
—Benjamin Franklin

"A goal without a plan is just a wish."
—Antoine de Saint-Exupery

"If you don't know where you're going, you'll end up someplace else."
—Yogi Berra

"It wasn't raining when Noah built the ark."
—Howard Ruff

Operating Rhythm

With a concept like ISR, it might be difficult to find practical application in your daily life. Too often people of faith use recycled intelligence. An example of this is our spiritual development. We become satisfied with living purely off of surveillance, but we fail at investigating and verifying beyond what we see. Many church attendees and church-staff members live exclusively off of the sermon they hear in church or on a podcast. This is their entire nutritional plan for spiritual sustenance. If your spiritual growth is based only on the analysis and opinions of others, you are at great risk of being captured by the enemy. When He was teaching His disciples to pray in Luke 11, Jesus said to ask God for "daily bread." It's possible He wasn't referring strictly to physical food but also spiritual food. We need fresh and daily bread. This means we need to digest God's word daily and ask the Holy Spirit to serve as our primary teacher. In Wayne Cordeiro's book *The Divine Mentor*, the author says, "Only you can keep yourself spiritually healthy by feeding yourself. No one can do it for you by proxy."

I'm stunned at how cavalier and reckless we are in the intelligence realm as men and women of faith. We would never buy a used car without analyzing price, maintenance history, gas mileage, or other facets. We research schools to every degree possible before deciding where we want to live. We spend countless hours checking reviews of VRBOs before committing vacation money. But we'll sit in a chair listening to a man teach from the Bible and take his version as God's truth. It's not only foolish but also contrary to what God says. The preacher can make a suggestion, but it is the Holy Spirit in me who makes decisions.

Technology and Tools

Superman could have used his powers for evil, but he chose to use them for good. AI is a tremendous resource that can assist in ISR. Synthesizing data, eliminating redundancy, detecting anomalies, and conducting research are only a few ways this tool can assist leaders. It is not a substitution or replacement for Godly wisdom, but it can provide information that informs our prayerful deliberation.

As an elder and, then, as senior leader in a large church for more than twenty years, I've experienced the value of ISR. I've also seen the ripples of failure that occur when it is ignored. I observed church leaders make countless staffing, hiring and other personnel decisions without fully employing sound ISR. They would choose a quick, less researched plan over a methodical and thorough approach. Sir Joshua Reynolds said, "There is no expedient to which a man will not resort to avoid the real labor of thinking." A failure to properly investigate has negative impact across many stakeholders. The ministry of the church suffers. The seeds of confusion are sown in the congregation due to leadership's failure. The other staff are adversely impacted. The individual who was improperly vetted is fired, reassigned, or resigns when they fail to meet expectations or previously known character flaws are revealed. Everyone loses when ISR is a rubber stamp.

The reasons why ISR is important to a leader—better timing, resource economy, risk management, tempo advantage, and trust and credibility—are applicable in every aspect of the church. From hiring staff to screening elders, deacons, and volunteer leaders, to making financial decisions about buildings and heavy maintenance, to evaluating whether to launch a new ministry or partner with an existing organization that serves this area are all perfect ways to use ISR in your operating rhythm. Decisions in the human-resources realm such as employee benefits, salary, performance reviews, and employee promotion, discipline, or termination are all better served when exposed to an ISR model.

ISR is not a department. It is a leadership discipline that fuses curiosity with rigor. Leaders who institutionalize ISR don't merely react faster; they choose better fights, commit resources at the decisive point, and maintain trust while doing it. In uncertain environments, the advantage goes to the leader who sees first, understands faster, and acts with justified confidence.

Application

Complete the self-audit below. Choose five to seven questions that highlight deficiencies and areas where the most risk exists. Turn them into a one-page ISR plan: requirements, sources, collection steps, indicators, and mitigations. Re-run the audit at six, nine, and twelve-month intervals to prevent drift.

Clarity of objective

- What is the exact outcome I'm aiming for, and how will I know it's done?
- What constraints are non-negotiable: time, budget, quality, scope?

Stakeholders and context

- Who is affected or accountable, and what do they need or expect?
- What prior decisions, norms, or politics shape this effort?

Information baseline

- What do I already know, what do I assume, and what evidence supports it?
- What critical unknowns could change the decision if clarified?

Research depth

- Have I identified primary sources, not just summaries?
- Did I consult at least two independent perspectives that might disagree?
- What relevant precedents, benchmarks, or case studies exist?

Ground truth and reconnaissance

- Have I observed the real environment or workflow where this will land?
- Did I talk to people closest to the problem, not just leaders or reports?
- What signals suggest that reality differs from the plan?

Risks and assumptions

- What are the top-three assumptions this plan rests on?
- What could go wrong with high impact, and how will I detect it early?

- What simple mitigations or contingencies are in place?

Options and trade-offs

- What are three viable alternatives, and why am I choosing this one?
- What am I explicitly not doing, and what trade-offs am I accepting?

Plan and sequencing

- Is the work broken into milestones with owners, dates, and exit criteria?
- What must be true before each milestone starts? What's the critical path?

Resourcing and feasibility

- Do I have the people, authority, budget, and tools required?
- What dependencies outside my control exist, and how will I secure them?

Small test before big bet

- What is the smallest experiment or pilot that could de-risk this?
- What evidence would cause me to stop, pivot, or scale?

Decision criteria

- What metrics or thresholds will guide go/no-go and success judgments?
- How will I collect the data in time to matter?

Communication and alignment

- Who needs to be informed or consulted, when, and with what cadence?
- Is there a clear single source of truth for scope and status?

Ethics, compliance, and reputation

- Does this plan meet legal, policy, and ethical standards?
- If made public, would the rationale hold up to scrutiny by those affected?

Readiness check

- If I had to start tomorrow, what would still be vague or missing?
- What would a skeptical peer challenge me on?

CHAPTER 8

★ ★ ★ ★ ★ ★ ★

Action

How much information do you need to act upon an idea? When a situation arises, how long do you study, analyze, and debate before you execute your formulated plan?

Sometimes you have to move before you get the whole picture. Sometimes you have to act before you even get the canvas. Some people yell "fire." Others run from the fire, but some are made to run into the fire.

On August 4, 2005, I woke up in my own bed and headed to the squadron. Our unit was rotating crews and airplanes to staging bases in Germany and Turkey in support of Operation Enduring Freedom and Operation Iraqi Freedom. I had recently returned home from my section's part of the deployment. While back at our home base, we were tasked with catching up on administrative duties, training objectives, and preparing for our next turn in "the sandbox," which was approximately thirty days away. It was great to be at home. Our daughters, Abby and Kate, were sixteen and thirteen, respectively, and school was still on hiatus for the summer. I was planning on a relatively short day and home in time for a family dinner, followed by family fun.

I was up and out before anyone else in the Wiggins house was moving around. I had an 0600 showtime for a local training mission. Several pilots needed to practice some of our mandated flight-currency items. *Air Force Manual 11-2C-17V1* is a 150-page document that defines and outlines every flight-currency item a pilot who flies a C-17 must accomplish. It explains how many takeoffs and landings must be performed each month, quarter, and year. It describes air-refueling requirements, night-vision goggle activities, instrument approaches, and air-drop procedures to perform. On this first Thursday in August, I was flying to meet some of those currency edicts. It was going to be a great and relatively easy day. Briefing was at 0600. Takeoff was at 0900. We'd fly directly to the rendezvous point to meet a KC-135 air-refueling aircraft. We'd take turns accomplishing in-flight refueling, and then, we'd head out for some low-level work. We'd fly a low-level route simulating we were navigating around enemy threats and egressing to an airfield, where we would perform several tactical approaches ultimately ending in a short-field landing. On a routine airlift mission, a pilot would land and gently ease off the brakes and exit the runway at a taxiway near the end of the airfield. A short-field landing is used to land either on a short runway or to land on only a portion of a runway. So, if the enemy bombed a segment of the runway, it would not adversely affect our operations. We could just land on the section that was intact. For the pilots, short-field landings are challenging and, candidly, lots of fun. For the passengers onboard, it's uncomfortable. The landings are firm, and the brakes are utilized to their design capabilities and limits. Depending on the weight of the aircraft, a normal landing might utilize 7,000 feet or more of runway. A short-field landing is defined as less than 3,500 feet. There's no smooth touchdown of the landing gear. There's no attempt to smoothly touch down or "grease it on." A pilot is looking for a solid and deliberate landing on an exact spot. After the short-field ops were concluded, we would fly back to Jackson, Mississippi, for some instrument-approach practice, culminating in a final landing at approximately 1400. After a debrief of the day and some administrative paperwork, I hoped to be in the car headed home by 1600.

Just prior to heading to the aircraft (called "stepping"), the command post called, asking that we delay at the squadron referred to by its building number, 240. A few minutes later, someone from our Current Operations office arrived at 240. Current Operations is the section that does what its name indicates: it plans all of the current operational missions. Their area of responsibility starts at home base and ends at the first landing location. After that, big Air Force takes over. The Current Ops chief wrangled our crew into a briefing room and explained that the Air Force called and was looking for a plane and a crew. Our instructions were to fly to New Orleans, and someone would meet us upon arrival.

We were not given any details other than "You might want to grab your go bag." Most military folks keep a "go bag." Some keep it in their car. Others maintain it in a locker at work. It contains varying items, depending on the individual's duty position and individual responsibilities. It usually contains five to seven days of clothes prepared for diverse climates and maybe a few MREs (meals ready to eat) or some dry snacks. You might throw in some extra batteries for flashlights and other items as well as a few personal things like a book to read or journal to write in. When I had arrived home from our latest deployment, I had pilfered my go bag. I will occasionally change out some of the clothes, and this time I had pulled a few things out and not replaced them. Fail. I called Jennabeth, and she brought me what I needed. She is always ready to react at a moment's notice. Everyone was back at the squadron in less than an hour, and we were ready to saddle up.

We departed Jackson for the forty-minute flight to New Orleans and Louis Armstrong International Airport. The airport name was changed in 2001 from its previous moniker of Moisant Field, which explains why the identifier for Louis Armstrong New Orleans International Airport is MSY, originally standing for Moisant Stock Yards which were co-located with the airport. Enroute to NOLA (New Orleans, Louisiana), we received additional information through our secure communications. A Russian Priz AS-28 mini-submarine, with 7 crew members onboard, was taking part in training exercises in Beryozovaya Bay, off the coast of Russia's far-eastern Kamchatka peninsula, when its propellers became entangled in cables that were part of Russia's coastal-monitoring system. Unable to surface, the sub was stranded in the dark, frigid waters 190 meters below the surface. They issued a mayday call. The Russian navy began to organize a rescue mission, soliciting help from Japan, the United Kingdom, and the United States. The accident occurred at 1300 local time (1:00 p.m.) on August 4 in Vladivostok, Russia, which would have been 2200 local time or 10:00 p.m. on August 3 in Jackson. We were flying to pick up a crew and their equipment from Phoenix International Underwater Solutions. Phoenix International provides manned and unmanned underwater operations and engineering services to civilian and military customers around the world. The Department of Defense contacted Phoenix International, asking if they would help rescue the sub crew. They agreed. All they needed was a ride from New Orleans to the far southeastern corner of Russia, which sits only 80 miles from the North Korean border. We were their ride. From the time we took off from Jackson, the sub crew had already been stranded for 12 hours.

We were scheduled to be on the ground in New Orleans for 3 hours. This would allow time to refuel, upload the cargo and passengers, and coordinate our flight plan. The flight plan was complex. In order to expedite our trip, we would fly direct from New Orleans to Vladivostok, Russia. A direct flight would take approximately 14 hours. Due to the weight of the cargo, the amount of fuel the plane could carry was limited, which would facilitate the need to conduct two air-refuelings. This required coordinating with two KC-10 tanker aircraft on rendezvous times and airspace to conduct the operation. Loading the cargo also proved problematic. Ultimately, we were on the ground for 6 hours, which required updating our flight plan and taking a further look at the weather we would encounter on the nearly 7,000-mile trip. It was 1700 (5:00 p.m. CST) when we departed. The sub crew had now been stranded for 19 hours.

The fact that the Russians asked for international assistance is a dramatic break from Kremlin practice and policy. The former Soviet bloc powers have always been secretive and protective of their governmental and military practices. You can point to many factors that might help explain their distrust and overly protective nature, but no factor is starker than the knowledge that 27 million Russians lost their lives in World War II. Compare that to 292,000 Americans, 450,000 from the United Kingdom, 3 million from Japan, and 7 million from Germany, and you can see the foundation of nationalism. The groundwork for their willingness to seek outside help had been laid 5 years earlier.

On August 12, 2000, the *Kursk*, a Russian nuclear-powered submarine, sank in the Barents Sea during a naval exercise. Crews of nearby vessels reported feeling 2 successive explosions. During an earlier mission, the *Kursk's* emergency locating beacon had been removed and was never reinstalled. This delayed search efforts. It took 16 hours to locate the *Kursk* and her crew of 118. After determining the vessel's location, several unsuccessful attempts were made to send rescue vehicles to attach to the emergency-escape hatch. The response was woefully slow and technically inept. During this time, the Russian government provided deliberately misleading information to the public and the family members of the crew. When the incident received international attention, the United States, Great Britain, Germany, France, and Israel were just a few of the nations that called Moscow, offering their assistance. All offers to help were refused. An August 14th statement from the Russian government stated the *Kursk* had experienced "minor technical difficulties," but rescuers were in touch with the crew of the *Kursk*.

After more failed attempts by the Russian navy, the Kremlin finally accepted international assistance from the British and Norwegian governments. On August 21, a British submersible and dive crews from both countries entered the wreckage of the *Kursk* to find the crew dead, all with severe burns, indicating they probably all died in one of the two explosions or the ensuing fire. Even after this discovery, Russia claimed that the accident was caused by a collision with a NATO vessel in the area. The backlash the government and the navy faced was unlike any public outcry both internal and external to the very private nation. Even the tightly controlled Russian media entity, *Pravda*, called the event a government conspiracy and took to task those responsible, calling for legal proceedings on behalf of the crew's families and the nation. With this still fresh on the minds of the nation's leaders, they clearly were more inclined to raise their hand and request aid.

The air-refueling portions of the mission were challenging. The weather was difficult. Visibility was adequate to locate the tanker aircraft at the rendezvous point and close to the contact position; however, after establishing contact, we were in continuous cloud cover for nearly the entire duration of both events. The KC-10 is a specially modified DC-10 aircraft. Its mission is to conduct air-refueling operations to extend the reach of other airplanes by eliminating the need to land and refuel. This operation saves significant time and closes the distance between an airplane's point of origin and its designated area of operation. It can carry three hundred fifty-six thousand pounds of fuel, or approximately fifty-three thousand gallons. Aircraft measure fuel in pounds, as the weight of the plane is a critical operational limit. The boom where the fuel is dispensed from the back of the aircraft is approximately thirty feet long. It has a limited range of motion both vertically and laterally. Each air refueling required that we onload approximately fifty-three thousand pounds of fuel. Based on the rate of transfer, we would need to be in the "contact," or fuel-receiving position, for about thirty minutes.

Imagine you're flying a large jet aircraft thirty feet or less from another large jet aircraft with mild turbulence bouncing both planes around. It's night, and the visibility decreases to the point where you can't even see the other plane's wings. You have to do all of this while flying your airplane in a space about the side of a two-car garage. Since our previously planned local mission had four pilots scheduled for flight training, we had some relief we would ordinarily not have onboard. I took the fuel during the first refueling. When the operation was complete, I noticed I was cold. It was because my flight suit was wet from the perspiration during the tense, roughly forty-minute ordeal. We successfully completed both refuelings and continued on our way to Russia.

We were told when we landed that we were the first American servicemen in Vladivostok since World War II. We were met by the Russian military and assisted as we offloaded the cargo and crew. The Phoenix team grabbed a bit of sleep during the fourteen-hour flight, so as they hit the ground, they were mildly fresh for their rescue operation. It was 1000 (10:00 a.m.) on August 5 in Jackson, Mississippi, and 0100 (1:00 a.m.) on August 6 in Vladivostok. The crew had been trapped for thirty-six hours.

It took several hours to complete post-flight inspections and service the plane for our departure at a time yet to be determined. We ultimately left the airport about 0600 (6:00 a.m.) for a ride to a Soviet-era military barracks. While we were thankful for the accommodations, they were spartan. The building had no heat, and the evening was a cool forty-five degrees. Also, it had no water. We took a nap for a couple of hours, but most of us couldn't sleep, so, at about noon, we decided to wander on foot into town.

When we arrived at a village outside of the city, it was obvious we were foreigners. The only Russian I knew was "*dosvedanya*," or "goodbye," which I'm sure I picked up from a movie. As we tried to communicate with the locals, it was clear they knew as much English as we did Russian. We were eventually directed to a bar that had a grill, and lunch was on our mind. Vodka might have been on the mind of some of our crew. There were several people in the bar, and they were watching television. The patrons were making some obvious and awkward glances in our direction. Pretty soon everybody in the bar was talking rather loudly and gesturing to us. The crowd came to our table and were emphatically talking to us with large hand motions, excited voices, and the occasional pat on the back. Eventually, they convinced us to stand and look at the television. While unable to understand the reporter, it was clear the rescue attempts had been successful and the seven men aboard the *Priz* were safe. What happened next was right out of Hollywood. The town descended on the bar, and we were the object of their affection and appreciation. After a few hours of eating and celebrating, we walked through the town to cheers and hugs of gratitude. There were several simultaneous rescue efforts in progress, and a British team had actually arrived on scene first and saved the crew. For the Russian people, if you had a part in the effort, you were lumped into the appreciation and accolades.

It's important to gather facts. In another part of this book, I elaborate on the importance of gathering intelligence, doing reconnaissance, and conducting mission planning. I've also written how critical it is to practice, conduct dry runs, mock drills, or rehearsals. Yet, all of those things are a complete waste of time if you don't act.

T. Boone Pickens said, "A plan without action is not a plan. It's a speech." Uncertainty swirls around our decision to act or not to act. Is it the right time? Do I have all the resources necessary? Am I the right person to meet this need? What if it goes wrong? What if I fail? What is the cost?

These questions are screaming for an answer, but if they are satisfied fully, the time to act will have come and gone. Andy Stanley is an author and pastor. He wrote, "You are probably never going to be more than about 80 percent certain." I guess that's true if you write books and pastor a large church in America, but that's poor theology and worse advice. Great men and women of the Bible like Noah, Abraham, David, Moses, Joshua, Ruth, Rahab, all the disciples, and Paul went through life with zero percent of the information but a small measure of faith. If they had 80 percent, where is the faith in that kind of obedience? There's not a mission I flew in the military that I had more than 50 percent of the information, and usually it hovered around 25 percent. The weather-briefing office at Naval Air Station Sigonella, Italy, had a round rock on the counter. When a pilot would arrive for the weather briefing for his mission, the instructions on the counter directed the pilot to spin the rock. The rock had the words "clear," "cloudy," "smooth," and "turbulent" painted on it. The pilot would spin the rock and whatever condition the arrow pointed to was your forecast. Just as you could never count on what the weather officer (aka weather guesser) predicted, the intelligence briefing about threats and local conditions was as predictable as a roulette wheel. According to stackexchange.com, if you spin a roulette wheel thirty-eight times, the probability is that it will land on red eighteen times, black eighteen times and green (0 or 00) two times. So, picking red on a roulette wheel gives you a 47 percent likelihood of success. BLUF is an acronym for "bottom line up front." When facing a decision to act, you will never have all the information you want and possibly even need; however, if you are presented the opportunity, God has given you the authorization to launch through His word in the Bible, through His spirit in you, or through wise and proven Godly counsel He's surrounded you with, it's time to move.

The uncertainty we faced in March 2005 was enormous. The State Department—*not* the Department of Defense was the lead agency. State is great at State stuff, but they are not operators and don't think or perform like people of my ilk. When we departed Jackson, we didn't have diplomatic clearance to fly into Russian airspace and certainly not to land in Russia. We didn't have the air-refueling tanker support needed to complete the mission. We were not sure of the precise weight of the cargo, which would affect aircraft performance, including fuel-burn rates. If we burned too much fuel enroute, we would not be able to reach and rendezvous with the tanker. If we couldn't refuel in flight, where would we divert to in order to land? Also, the weather changed significantly over the thirty-six hours of the mission from notification to landing in Russia. Lastly, just to fly the mission, we were violating every portion of Air Force Instruction 11-202, Flying Operations; General Flight Rules. We were asked if we could fly the mission. We were not ordered to, so anything that went wrong was going to hang on the crew for disobeying Air Force Regulations.

So, what's the advice? At the end of the day, how do you know what to do when you're in a position to act?

Pray

Prayer is considered the right answer and the church answer. Tossing a prayer toward heaven when you're aware of a difficult situation, making a decision, and seeking God's blessing on your plan is our general approach to prayer. This is like having a flashlight in your hand but the batteries in your pocket. If you want the flashlight to illuminate something, you should insert the batteries first. A faith-filled life is powered by prayer that is constant. Was I praying on August 4 and 5, 2005, as I executed this mission? Absolutely. But, those prayers were powered by meditation that occurred days, weeks, months, and years earlier, asking for God's wisdom, providence, grace, and His spiritual fruit. In prayer, God's spirit will point you to His word, and His word will point you back to Him.

The Bible is full of examples of people who put this into practice. Moses said that, if God's presence does not go with them, they should not go (Exodus 33:15). Elijah prayed as he battled on Mount Carmel (1 Kings 18:36). King Hezekiah was sick, so he sought God through prayer (2 Kings 20:1–6). Joshua assembled an army and went up against 5 kings (Joshua 10:11–14). Before Jesus selected the 12 disciples, he prayed all night (Luke 6:12). Peter was locked in prison, and his friends needed an answer (Acts 12:1–17).

Prayer isn't the backup plan. Prayer is the primary plan, and it's best employed foundationally rather than as a wreath on the front door after you finished building your house of response.

Experience

When the rescue-mission opportunity was presented, I was an 18-year Air Force veteran. I had amassed nearly 5,000 flight hours and 250 hours of combat time. I had flown air-refueling missions on countless occasions. I had flown to Russia previously as part of an inspection team tasked with observing the country's compliance with the 1987 Intermediate-Range Nuclear Forces Treaty (INF). I had encountered many of the challenges we would face, but not all of them. Our crew of 4 pilots and 2 loadmasters combined for 82 years of flying experience. So, as the commander of this mission, I didn't have to have all of the answers. I just needed to tap into the other 64 years worth of life in order to either find the answer or develop the best solution available. In his book *Win the Day*, pastor and author Mark Batterson recalls his desire to write his first book. Yet, he lacked practical training and maturity. As Batterson tells the story, "When I felt called to write, I started reading about two hundred books a year. Many people find that hard to believe, but I was pastoring nineteen people our first year! I had some time on my hands. But, I didn't just find time. I made time. We didn't have smart phones or social media. This alone adds hours back into the day! What inspired me? I heard that the average author puts about two years of life experience into a book. At twenty-five, life experience is what I was lacking! I did the math. If I read two hundred books in a year, I'd gain four hundred years of life experience." You might not commit to reading two hundred books in a year, but I'll bet you could read twenty-four—or two books a month. That would add nearly fifty years of experience to your life annually. When it's time to act, use your experience. Use the experience of those around you. Use the experience of the people you have read. You don't have to be an eighteen-year veteran of anything to act. You just have to be willing and admit, like the rest of us, that you don't have all of the answers.

Preparation/Practice

Winston Churchill said, "To each, there comes in their lifetime a special moment when they are figuratively tapped on the shoulder and offered the chance to do a very special thing, unique to them and fitted to their talents. What a tragedy if that moment finds them unprepared or unqualified for what could have been their finest hour." Action that is not proceeded by preparation is usually bravado that leads to failure. The Greek philosopher Epictetus said that, when facing adversity, we should be able to say, "This is what I've trained for. Life has twists and turns for us. Our job is to be ready."

Courage

Ryan Holiday's book *Courage Is Calling* is a call-to-arms *to act*. He does a masterful job of highlighting the challenges to acting courageously and actions necessary to stride toward resolve and commitment. He writes, "It is essential that we understand that courage is more than just the stand. It's more than just the choice of Hercules, between the easy road and the hard one. One then has to walk the hard road." Courage is not for a moment; it is a choice of a lifetime. It's confronting the bully and being honest on your taxes. It's admitting your error and standing against your best friend or boss when they are wrong. Courage is often in conflict with popularity and frequently calls you to stand alone. The Bible says the wide road leads to destruction but the narrow path leads to righteousness. Action requires a teaspoon of courage to start, and it demands an ocean to stay committed to completion.

Leadership is revealed in the split second after the metaphorical grenade lands. Some will run, prioritizing self-preservation over team outcomes. Some will freeze, paralyzed by uncertainty and the fear of choosing wrong. Others will jump on the grenade, absorbing risk to protect others—a noble instinct that can prevent immediate damage but may not solve the underlying problem. The rarest leaders pick it up and throw it back: they stay calm, assess the threat, act decisively, and turn disruption into momentum. Great leadership blends all four impulses with judgment—courage to shield, composure to think, and the strategic clarity to neutralize the source—so that the team not only survives the blast but also learns to face the next one with confidence.

Action might be the tip end of the spear, but the shaft is built with prayer, experience, preparation, and courage. Social media glamorizes the outcome, but action isn't built on selfies, likes, and reposts. Action is delivered by the constant crucible of prayer, experience, practice/

preparation, and courage. Jesus didn't seek comfort. He stepped toward chaos. Leaders in the church should follow His example and be bent toward action that disrupts the status quo of religion.

Application

Ask yourself the questions below to raise your awareness of your leanings to timely and appropriate action versus passive and fearful responses. When you feel stuck or anxious, answer five questions: one from Timing, one from Decision Clarity, one from Appropriateness, one from Stakeholders, one from Courage. Write a three-line action card: Intent, First step, Trigger to pivot. Execute within the hour. Review weekly: note one moment you acted timely and one you delayed, and extract a rule you'll apply next time.

Situation sensing

- What exactly changed that requires action now?
- What is the mission-critical outcome, and what "good enough" result is acceptable today?

Bias and fear check

- What am I afraid will happen if I act? If I don't act?
- Is this risk real and material, or imagined and reputational?
- What evidence contradicts my fear?

Decision clarity

- What is the smallest decisive action that advances the goal?

- What options exist right now? Which is reversible and buys information fast?
- If I do nothing for twenty-four hours, what worsens or closes?

Timing and thresholds

- What indicators make this a "go," "no-go," or "wait" situation?
- What deadline or window am I operating under, and who set it?
- What is the cost of delay vs. the cost of acting imperfectly?

Appropriateness and safeguards

- What constraints must I respect: legal, ethical, policy, safety?
- What's the minimum viable action that is safe, compliant, and useful?
- What guardrails will prevent overreach or escalation?

Stakeholders and communication

- Who needs to know now, and what do they need to decide or act on?
- What is the simplest clear message I can send in the next ten minutes?
- Who can sanity-check my plan quickly?

Resources and authority

- Do I have the access, skills, and remit to act? If not, who does?
- What support or escalation path is available if this widens?

Execution plan (one page)

- What will I do in the next fifteen minutes, next two hours, next day?
- What's the trigger to stop, pivot, or escalate?
- How will I capture signals to learn while acting?

Courage vs. recklessness

- Am I choosing short-term discomfort to protect long-term outcomes?
- What prudent step makes this action bold but not blind?

After-action loop

- What result did I get, and what did I learn?
- What will I adjust before the next decision point?

CHAPTER 9

★★★★★★★

Dealing with Failure

I taxied onto the runway at Williams Air Force Base, Phoenix, Arizona. It was my second evaluation in Air Force Undergraduate Pilot Training (UPT). I had survived the ninety-minute oral evaluation from the examiner pilot (EP) as well as the academic testing on aircraft systems, Federal Aviation Administration (FAA) flight rules, *Air Force Manual 51-37 Instrument Flying* testing as well as completing, without error, the aircraft emergency-procedures test affectionately known as a "Bold Face" test. (The text for emergency procedures immediate action is written in bold print; therefore, it's called "bold face" among pilots.) Now, all I had to do was fly the prescribed maneuvers over the next hour and fifteen minutes while the EP watched and annotated everything I did.

I completed the Before Takeoff and Lineup Checklists, and the control tower cleared me for takeoff. I advanced the throttles to takeoff power and released the brakes.

"I have the aircraft." Those words that came across the aircraft-interphone system were alarming. The EP watches—but rarely says a word. For him to speak and take control of the aircraft meant there was a problem—and, apparently, a problem I was unaware of. As a pilot, being unaware of a problem is not acceptable.

The EP kept control of the T-37 aircraft. He taxied the plane down the runway, pulled off, and took us back to parking. He performed the Engine Shutdown Checklist. Then, he spoke again. "What is the allowable altimeter error between a known checkpoint and what the altimeter indicates?"

The altimeter is an instrument in the cockpit of an airplane that measures the height of an aircraft above a fixed level. Bottom line, it tells the pilot how high above the ground the airplane is. So, if the air traffic controller issues instructions such as, "Climb to 10,000 feet," the pilot uses the altimeter to correctly identify the altitude. An altimeter is allowed to have a slight variance. The allowable error of +/- 75 feet of deviation.

In the T-37, the pilot is required to check the altimeter deviation during the "Line Up" check that is performed just prior to beginning your takeoff run or while you're lining up on the runway. There was a sign at Wiliams AFB that indicated the end of the runway was 1,374 feet MSL. The altimeter on a T-37 was a standard Falcon 3⅛-inch sensitive altimeter. If you picture a clock face where the numbers from 1 to 12 are placed on the outside of the clock, and there are hash marks between the numbers indicating minutes, this altimeter is very similar. The numbers run from 0 to 9, and there are 4 hash marks between each number. The size of the instrument is 3 ⅛-inches in diameter. The altimeter is nearly centered to the right side of the pilot who occupies the left seat. The EP sits in the right seat. So, the EP sees the instrument at an angle while the pilot in the left seat (me, in this case) is looking directly at it.

When I looked at the altimeter during the checklist, the needle pointed just beyond the 1,300 feet indication. As I mentioned, the gauge would give you a clear indication of 1,300 feet. Between

1,300 feet and 1,400 feet, there are 4 slashes representing 20-feet increments. The needle on the altimeter was between 1,300 feet and 1,320 feet. While close to being outside of tolerances, it was allowable. I answered the examiner that the altimeter at the checkpoint read "approximately 1,320 feet."

He responded, "From my vantage point, it looked just below 1,300 feet."

I knew what that meant: I'd failed the evaluation before the aircraft ever left the runway.

We changed airplanes and started the process all over again. I flew a near-flawless sortie. We landed and returned to the flight room to debrief the flight. The EP gave me great reviews for my testing, academic knowledge, and all flight maneuvers with some minor variations. Then, he said that, despite all of those areas of excellence, the evaluation was considered a failure. In pilot training, we called it "a bust." It was a bust for one item: failure to know the allowable error of the altimeter.

I was humiliated and incensed by what had happened. I knew the regulations. I completed the checklist properly. A guy sitting with an obstructed view of a 4-inches-in-diameter instrument thought he could see it better than me. When you fail a check ride, you have to re-accomplish the items you failed to meet standards. My makeup evaluation required me to see the Chief of Standardization and have him ask me one question. "Lieutenant Wiggins, what is the allowable error of the aircraft altimeter from a known checkpoint?" I responded, "Plus or minus 75 feet"—the same answer I gave the day of the evaluation. He looked at me. "This was a waste of Air Force resources. You've passed. Congratulations."

My aviation record was now saddled with what is known in Air Force circles as a "Q3." Q1 is an indication of fully qualified. Q2 is qualified with some restrictions. Q3 is unqualified. The sum total of this event is listed on my pilot-training record as "Q3/Q1." In essence, I failed but passed the re-make.

I knew the EP was wrong. Even the Chief of Standardization told me as much; however, it didn't matter. I failed, and now, I had to determine my response to failure. Air Force-pilot training is an incredibly intense fifty-two weeks of work. Most days are sixteen-plus hours. When the day is over, there's more studying required to be prepared for the next day. When I attended UPT, the failure rate known as the "wash-out rate" was approximately 30 percent. Even prior to attending UPT, screening disqualifies more than 75 percent of the applicants. It's an elite lot who get the opportunity to one day wear the Air Force's silver wings indicating you're a pilot. When someone fails a flight evaluation, an academic test, or other marker of required success, it is almost like blood in the water. Instructors take a more personal interest in you—not to console, coddle, or encourage you, but rather test you to see if you will recover. Oftentimes, a singular failure leads a trainee on a downward spiral from which is unrecoverable. Before you know it, you see your former classmate in "casual status," which is a transitional phase, where the Air Force determines if you will be allowed to cross-train to a different career field or return you to civilian life. If you imagine the life of a leper in the scriptures, you have a perfect image of "casual status."

Wearing the stigma of failure as I came home that night, I told Jennabeth about the day. At this time, we had been married for five years. Our first daughter, Abby was four months old. I was a full-time student pilot and barely a part-time husband or Dad. In the midst of the chaos of her day, Jennabeth affirmed that I had the right stuff to be an Air Force pilot and asked what she could do to help. Besides doing everything for the house, us, and Abby, Jennabeth was my study partner. She quizzed me about aircraft systems, graded my tests, and listened to me fly an imaginary airplane from the side of the bed as I looked at a poster of the cockpit of a T-37. Jennabeth would have aced pilot training, except for the fact that following orders without being able to ask "Why?" is not her strong suit.

Our response to failure needs to take on several actions. An "Ace" in the Air Force is a pilot who has shot down five enemy aircraft. We need to be an Ace in our response to failure. There are potential enemies to our recovery. I've identified five areas we need to address in order to step beyond failure. Each starts with the letter "A."

Attitude

Our response to failure starts with our attitude. It also ends with attitude. Attitude must be sprinkled into every movement as we walk through failure. Psychologist Carol Dweck found that people's core attitudes fall into one of two categories: a fixed mindset or a growth mindset. With a fixed mindset, you believe you are who you are and that you cannot change. This creates problems when you're challenged, because anything that appears to be more than you can handle is bound to make you feel hopeless and overwhelmed. People with a growth mindset believe that they can improve with effort. They outperform those with a fixed mindset, even when they have a lower IQ, because they embrace challenges, treating them as opportunities to learn something new. Dweck says success in life is all about how you deal with failure. She describes the approach to failure of people with the growth mindset this way: "Failure is information—we label it 'failure,' but it's more like, 'This didn't work, and I'm a problem-solver, so I'll try something else.'" Common sense would suggest that having ability, like being smart, inspires confidence. It does—but only while the going is easy. The deciding factor in life is how you handle setbacks and challenges. People with a growth mindset welcome setbacks with open arms."

The Apostle Paul would agree that our focus, our mind, our attitude is key. "Finally, brethren, whatever is true, whatever is honorable, whatever is right, whatever is pure, whatever is lovely, whatever is of good repute, if there is any excellence and, if anything worthy of praise, dwell on these things" (Philippians 4:8, NASB). He didn't say to dwell on failure or how you were wronged or the fairness of the outcome. He said to concentrate on the lessons learned, the growth opportunity, and the path ahead.

Acceptance/Acknowledgment

In Ryan Holiday's book *The Obstacle Is the Way*, he says, "We decide what story to tell ourselves. Or whether we will tell one at all." We have to tell ourselves the truth. In recognizing the reality of failure, we step toward acknowledgment and acceptance. Failure may be a comma, period, next paragraph, or possibly a new book. Regardless, you must embrace the transition to the next. If you don't admit you're lost, you will never be found. George Washington lost more battles than he won, yet he learned from each failure and fashioned victory as a response.

Aptitude

Anytime there is an aircraft accident in the Air Force, a Safety Investigation Board (SIB) is convened. This board is led by a board president, usually a Colonel, and several subject-matter experts are a part of the group. The experts range in areas of responsibility from medical (flight surgeon), to a recorder (handles the administrative functions), to a flight safety officer, and someone who is highly qualified in the weapons system (aircraft) that was involved in the accident. These subject-matter experts (SMEs) are charged with using their in-depth knowledge in their specific realm to help prevent future accidents. As an SME, you are constantly adding to your reservoir of knowledge through additional Air Force resources but also through personal study and investigation. An SME doesn't attend formal school training, and, then, stops learning. They are always on a quest to add to their acumen. Lives are at stake.

A key component in bouncing back from failure is figuratively going back to school. President Harry Truman said, "It's what you learn after you know it all that counts." Failure itself is not the teacher. The education comes from continual study, the acquisition of knowledge, and game experience in your chosen field of pursuit. In the local church, I'm appalled at the lack of professional growth I see in most pastors. It appears that a degree, whether from a secular university or seminary—or both—comes with a clause that relieves the holder of any future duty to advancement. Pastors should set the example in theological growth, but that's not all. Leaders in the church should grow in their understanding of the culture they are called to shepherd. During interviews for positions on our ministerial staff, I'll often ask questions about current events. "Give me a synopsis of the DOW Industrial over the past year." "Who is the Secretary of State?" "Tell me the title of a book you've read from the *New York Times* Bestseller List." "What are the most pressing issues kids, college students, young adults, parents, and senior adults are facing?" I guarantee the folks in your church know the answers. If you want to connect, you need to grow in your aptitude of current culture.

Aspiration/Appetite

Albert Einstein said, "You never fail until you stop trying." Your response to failure should be to aspire to the next thing. There are countless examples of people who responded to failure by aspiring to the next challenge. Abraham Lincoln lost more elections than he won. Author J.K. Rowling describes herself as ". . . failing on an epic scale. An exceptionally short-lived marriage had imploded, and I was jobless, a lone parent, and as poor as it is possible to be in modern Britain, without being homeless. The fears that my parents had had for me, and that I had had for myself, had both come to pass, and by every usual standard, I was the biggest failure I knew." Ms. Rowling aspired to something more, and the *Harry Potter* book and movie-ticket purchases from the Wiggins house alone have set her up for success for years to come.

Aspiration in the local church can present challenges. On one hand, you love to see people who seek new challenges. In Patrick Lencioni's book *The Ideal Team Player*, he says, "The kind of people that all teams need are people who are humble, hungry, and smart. . . . Hungry, meaning they have a strong work ethic, are determined to get things done, and contribute any way they can." Yet, this quality must be balanced with a commitment to the position you have versus the one you desire. Nothing is more frustrating and more toxic than a minister who is continually looking for his next role rather than fully serving in the current position. First Peter 5:6 gives us the proper perspective: "Therefore humble yourselves under the mighty hand of God, that He may exalt you at the proper time." When a new role does come, pastors too often take an attitude of arrival rather than a continued hungry pursuit of growth. The military has a term for this—"ROAD" or "Retired on Active Duty." It describes someone who has reached their final position or promotion and intend to serve without passion or distinction the remainder of their days until they leave the service. All Christians are called to run the race of life as Paul describes in 2 Timothy 4:7: "I have fought the good fight, I have finished the course, I have kept the faith"; and as you are running, "Run in such a way that you may win" (1 Corinthians 9:24). Ultimately, aspire to *be more* rather than just *do more.*

To desire or to aspire has a heady, theoretical connotation. The kind of aspiration I'm talking about has perspiration and grit. It has an appetite. In order to rebound from failure, you have to have tenacity to reach the new or next goal. Perhaps no organization exemplifies this kind of aggression better than the National Aeronautics and Space Administration (NASA). Twenty-two months after the deaths of three astronauts in the Apollo 1 disaster during a training exercise on the launch pad, Apollo 8 circled the moon ten times. Nine months after Apollo 13 had to cut its mission short, Apollo 14 landed on the moon. The space shuttle *Discovery* launched just eight months after the *Challenger* disaster. No matter the obstacle, NASA continued with zeal to complete the mission.

Leaders in the church have plenty of opportunity to display grit. The same sermon is too long and not long enough. The message is not deep enough for some and too jammed full of abstract and useless theological references for others. Student pastors are too friendly with some students and not connected appropriately with others. Worship pastors lead in environments that are too loud, not loud enough, too contemporary or too old-fashioned, all while wearing skinny jeans with too many tattoos. A great response to criticism and failure is in Matthew 22:37–38: "Jesus replied: 'Love the Lord your God with all your heart and with all your soul and with all your mind.' This is the first and greatest commandment. And the second is like it: 'Love your neighbor as yourself.'" After you deploy these, then, be aggressive in showing some grit.

Nobody bounced back from failure better than the Apostle Peter. After denying he knew Jesus three times, Peter had quite a comeback. He assumed the leadership of the disciples and the early church. He traveled from Jerusalem to Antioch, Ephesus, Corinth, and Rome. He once cowered at the claims of a teenage girl, but after being forgiven and restored by Jesus, he preached the gospel message in such a way that it echoes through history to our ears today.

Accountability

With Attitude, Acceptance, and Aspiration in your tank, it's time to forge ahead. When I administered flight evaluations, I would tell the examinee, in the briefing prior to starting, that they were going to make mistakes. They were going to give an incorrect answer in the oral portion. They would miss a question on the written segment. They will also incorrectly perform a procedure in the aircraft. Most of the time, none of these things will result in an unsatisfactory grade. However, if they live in the past or loiter over the mistake, this distraction will cause a lack of attention to detail in other areas and create additional mistakes, which can result in an unsatisfactory result. It's vital to learn from the error and, then, FIAMO . . . forget it and move on.

As you move on, adding another set of eyes, ears, and analysis is helpful and healthy. Introducing accountability into your pursuits is a great tool for adding to the potential of future success. Mentors and coaches can be a part of your personal training-and-development system. Not all mentors and coaches are created equal. As you consider someone, some keys to look for are:

- **Model.** Is this someone you want to model?
- **Available and Consistent.** Are they willing to commit to an agreed-upon schedule and duration?
- **Success.** Do they have a record of success in the area(s) you're seeking growth in?
- **Present.** They need to be physically present in your life. A mentor who rarely sees you and is geographically separated is called "a consultant." Accountability isn't a consultation; it's a mandate based upon mutually agreed-to values and goals.

- **Credibility.** Do they follow the advice they give others?
- **Trustworthy.** Do they keep a confidence?

Also, don't expect gaining a mentor or coach to be a one-stop-shopping event. They might not be the person you're seeking for encouragement or affirmation. They might not possess the right "how" when it comes to your specific gifts and talents. It's a buffet; select what you like, but don't forget to eat your vegetables. Green Skittles are not a vegetable.

Dealing with failure isn't a singular lesson that you learn and move on from forever. When you choose to do something hard, when you decide to tackle a challenge that is contrary to culture, when you're willing to stand alone against a vast sea of contrarians, failure will continually visit you. Sometimes bouncing back from these occurrences is more than a mental pep talk. Sometimes the road back takes years. I've had such a journey, and it started in October 1993.

Somalia is a country in western Africa. To the east, it is bordered by Ethiopia and Kenya. The Arabian Sea is to the west. For the last several decades, Somalia has been ravaged by the effects of civil war. One iteration of that violence started in the late 1980s and spilled over into the 1990s. The humanitarian crisis that accompanied the war was vast. In 1992, President George H. W. Bush announced the U.S. military would assist in a multinational relief effort to assist the citizens of Somalia. Despite the efforts, the food and medical supplies did not provide the necessary relief as the faction leaders hijacked most of the goods and sold them to neighboring countries and militias for weapons. In December 1992, the United States changed its strategy.

Operation Restore Hope was launched in December 1992. In addition to airlift resources, the U.S. committed troops to the United Nations' operation to provide security for the supplies. Bolstered by the Marines, Army, and Air Force, supplies started to arrive to the sick and starving. This provided needed stability to the country, which, in turn, served as a catalyst for U.N.-sponsored negotiations in March 1993 between warring factions in Somalia. For the first time in decades, there was hope for peace.

Optimism evaporated on June 5, 1993. A group of Somali militia, led by Mohamed Farrah Aidid, attached a predominantly Pakistani U.N. force who were inspecting a weapons cache. The attack resulted in twenty-four dead and sixty wounded U.N. personnel, including an Italian soldier and three Americans. The U.N. responded by issuing a warrant for the arrest of Aidid.

Intelligence reports indicated that many of Aidid's top lieutenants were going to be at a meeting in Mogadishu, Somalia. On July 12, 1993, the U.S. led an attack on this meeting location. The attack was labeled "Bloody Monday," as estimates say more than two hundred people were killed, including members of the militia as well as civilians. Despite tensions continuing to rise, the U.S. troop strength decreased from a high of twenty-five thousand to about twelve hundred by the end of July.

Things reached the boiling point in October 1993. Intelligence reports indicated Aidid was going to be at a meeting location. Plans were made to capture him. U.S. Army Delta Force personnel were supported by Black Hawk helicopters. What ensued became known as *Black Hawk Down* as two helicopters were shot down. U.S. forces were significantly outnumbered. Delta Force set up defensive positions around the crash sites, but when reinforcements arrived, things had already turned deadly. In the end, eighteen Americans were killed and seventy-three wounded. Video images ran on news outlets around the world, punctuated by the body of U.S. Army Staff Sergeant William David Cleveland being dragged through the streets of Mogadishu.

There's an academic part of failure. You have a task, responsibility, or mission with a desired outcome. If you don't achieve your expected results, you label it as failure. As you conduct the post-mortem, you consider your attitude, aspiration, acknowledgment, aptitude, and accountability as you move forward. Failure has another part that is insidious. It's how it attacks you emotionally. Failure can lead you to "stinkin' thinkin'." Doubt creeps into your mind. Then, guilt takes a shot at your identity. Lastly, shame brings to bear an overarching paralysis that moves you from the outcome of an activity to a cloak you adopt as a burial shroud.

I was a part of Operation Restore Hope. Academically, I know there is nothing I could have done to change the outcome of October 3–4, 1993. Emotionally, I've carried guilt and shame for more than thirty years. Why did Corporal Jamie Smith not come home? Why did I return to my wife and daughters while the families of CW3 Bull Briley and CW4 Ironman Frank would live the rest of their lives without their husband, father, brother, son? Where is the justice for these men? And, as you look at Somalia in the years following, including the embassy attack in Benghazi in 2012 that killed four Americans and injured three others, what good came of it all?

After failing that flight evaluation in pilot training, I rallied. With great support from Jennabeth and utilizing the "A" values, not only did I receive my pilot wings in 1990, but I was also awarded the "Top Officer" trophy at graduation, given to the student that most exemplified the values of the Air Force. While I don't know all of the reasons why the instructor pilots selected me for this honor, I believe refusing to accept failure was part of their assessment. As for the failure in Somalia, I'm still a work in progress. I'm better than I was yesterday, but I hope for newfound freedom tomorrow. I've learned from failure, and I'm determined that I will not be defined by it. Many more failures will come as well as many more opportunities to display resilience. I agree with former Vice President Hubert Humphrey's saying, "Never give in, and never give up."

Application

Ask yourself these questions to analyze your response to failure. Are you minimizing or overly critical of the outcome?

Reality check

- Have I stated plainly what failed, without spin or blame?
- What was the expected outcome vs. the actual, with dates and facts?

Ownership

- What part is unequivocally mine to own?
- What actions am I taking now, without waiting for others?

Emotional regulation

- What emotions am I feeling, and am I processing them productively?
- Am I avoiding shame spirals or defensiveness that block learning?

Stakeholder care

- Who is affected, and what do they need right now?
- Have I communicated early, candidly, and with a path forward?

Repair and mitigation

- What immediate steps can I take to reduce harm or prevent further loss?
- What can be salvaged, repurposed, or delivered as a partial win?

Root cause

- What are the proximate causes and the deeper, systemic causes?
- Which causes are controllable vs. contextual? How do I know?

Learning and change

- What one to three behaviors, processes, or guardrails will I change next time?
- How will I test that the change actually prevents recurrence?

Decision and timing

- Is this a fix, pivot, or stop moment? What criteria guide that call?
- What indicators would tell me to change course sooner next time?

Communication quality

- Did I share the right level of detail, at the right time, with the right tone?
- Did I close the loop when new info emerged or the situation resolved?

Team and culture

- Did I invite candid feedback and dissenting views?
- Am I modeling a response that makes it safer for others to surface issues early?

Integrity and fairness

- Have I avoided scapegoating and credited others' efforts accurately?
- Am I applying the same standards to myself that I apply to others?

Perspective and resilience

- What does this failure teach that success could not?
- What remains in my control today that moves things one step forward?

Metrics and evidence

- What measurable signals show the issue is resolved?
- What metric will I monitor for the next four to six weeks to catch regressions?

Exit and after-action

- What will I capture for an after-action review?
- What is the one sentence I want to remember from this failure?

CHAPTER 10

★★★★★★★

Delegation

"Bucket List" is a relatively common term. It refers to goals someone wants to accomplish in their lifetime or before they "kick the bucket." The phrase gained wider exposure and was introduced to a new generation with the release of the 2007 movie *The Bucket List*, starring Morgan Freeman and Jack Nicholson.

The movie follows two terminally ill men from very different worlds—billionaire hospital tycoon Edward Cole, played by Nicholson, and blue-collar mechanic Carter Chambers, played by Freeman—who meet in a cancer ward and decide to spend their remaining months completing a shared "bucket list" of life-affirming adventures. As they race from skydiving and racing cars to visiting the pyramids and the Taj Mahal, their unlikely friendship deepens, forcing each to confront regrets, reconcile with family, and redefine what a meaningful life looks like. Their journey blends humor with poignancy, suggesting that joy, forgiveness, and authentic connection matter more than wealth or status, and that it's never too late to live with purpose.

I haven't been intentional about compiling a bucket list. When I received my pilot wings following graduation for the Air Force's Undergraduate Pilot Training (UPT), I knew that was one of the mountains I wanted to climb. After flying for a few years, a second dream came into focus.

Commanding an Air Force flying squadron is a defining accomplishment for a pilot. Leading an organization of approximately two hundred airmen to accomplish the mission assigned by the Air Force is everything Edward Cole and Carter Chambers did in the movie all rolled into one. The privilege of command and the honor of overseeing your fellow aviators is like receiving a gift you don't deserve and could never earn. I was presented that gift when I became the 183rd Airlift Squadron Commander of the 172nd Air Wing.

As a Lieutenant Colonel at the time, I was not the most senior-in-rank pilot. My operational-pilot evaluations were all satisfactory, but I didn't see myself as the "top stick" or best pilot in the unit. My officer performance reviews were at the top of my peers, but, to use common vernacular, I wasn't the G.O.A.T. (Greatest of All Time). Yet, for some reason, I was offered the position, and I accepted with some apprehension but also limitless excitement. The timing of my appointment was a weighty part of the opportunity. The United States was five years into Operation Enduring Freedom and Operation Iraqi Freedom. We deployed continuously fighting the war on terror, and I was going to continue that tempo, leading the squadron in combat operations. General Douglas MacArthur said, "The soldier above all prays for peace, for it is the soldier who must suffer and bear the deepest wounds and scars of war."

Assuming the helm of the 183rd AS was like becoming the coach of the reigning Super Bowl or World Series champions. The squadron was stacked with all-star talent. The unit had recently transitioned to C-17 aircraft, and several elite pilots made the move from the active-duty Air Force to join our Air National Guard wing. Barry Blanchard, Mike Sparrow, Todd Baker, Mike Singer, and Jon Reesman led this group and were widely considered experts in the weapon system. Add established unit pilots with vast experience like Judd Moss, Nap Bryan, and James Hartline, and we were flush with some of the best aviators in the world. But wait—there's more. The loadmaster contingency was even more well represented with military and flight experience. Allen Randall, Johnny Gressett, Ricky Davis, Shane Griffith, Chris Henderson, and Brian Hamilton had a work ethic that was exceeded only by their wisdom. My job was to coach the Dream Team.

The principles of command are outlined in *Air Force Doctrine Publication 1-1.* They include:

- **Commander's Intent.** A clear, concise statement of the operation's purpose, desired end state, and what must be accomplished—not how—nested within higher intent, including expectations, constraints, restraints, risks, and mission purpose.
- **Competence.** Proficiency in duties and a commitment to tactical, technical, and intellectual self-improvement, deliberately developed through education, training, and experience. Consistently observed competence builds trust.
- **Mutual Trust.** Shared confidence among commanders, subordinates, and partners based on demonstrated reliability, competence, integrity, and shared experience. It is earned over time and eroded by incompetence, dishonesty, or pridefulness.
- **Shared Understanding.** A common awareness and comprehension of the operational environment, organizational competence and limits, and how each role contributes to mission success, built through clear, two-way communication and feedback.
- **Risk Acceptance.** Skillful assessment and acceptance of risk, balancing force protection with mission accomplishment, with risk tolerance tied to competence and clearly communicated

across echelons to prevent unwarranted or strategically harmful risk-taking.

- **Mission Orders.** A technique for writing orders that focuses on purpose and outcomes rather than details how to perform tasks, specifying authorities, and empowering maximum freedom of action within commander's intent. Using MTOs alone does not equal mission command.
- **Disciplined Initiative.** Proactive inventiveness and creativity when orders no longer fit or unforeseen threats or opportunities arise, bounded by commander's intent and the broader operational and strategic context.

The Air Force applies these principles with centralized command, distributed control, and decentralized execution. Senior commanders retain command authority, while control and execution are pushed as far forward as practical, so that Airmen can act rapidly within the commander's intent.

While this word salad of military jargon might lose you, these principles were the air that we breathed. They are as common as an accountant balancing a spreadsheet, an attorney reviewing a contract, or a dental hygienist cleaning a patient's teeth. Due to instruction, practice, and years of repetition, knowing *what* to do was easy. When you're commanding the Dream Team, the hard part was determining *how* to do it.

Despite being surrounded by people with more military experience, officers who were more senior, and aviators with hundreds of more flight hours, I was charged with leading this organization and effectively wielding this weapon. I had to learn how to command through effective delegation while avoiding abdicating to others. The road was bumpy at times. My learning to lead at this level had a price that was often paid by the men and women I led. Due to their commitment and competence, my tenure as the commander was successfully affirmed by the unit receiving countless awards, maintaining a standard-setting mission-capable rate, flying a record number of mishap-free combat hours, and individual squadron members receiving military decorations for heroism and meritorious service.

Part of our success can be attributed to my understanding and growth in differentiating between delegating and abdicating. Below is a framework to help you analyze and, if necessary, adapt your behavior.

Delegation Scorecard

1. **Choose the right work to delegate**
   - Delegate outcomes, not just tasks. Give projects that grow skills and free up your time for higher-leverage work.
   - Keep mission-critical, sensitive, or uniquely expert work for yourself.
2. **Match task to person**
   - Align difficulty with capability and growth goals.
   - Clarify why you chose them, to build ownership.
3. **Define success clearly**
   - State the desired outcome, constraints, non-negotiables, and decision boundaries.
   - Share context: stakeholders, dependencies, risks, and what "good" looks like.
   - Agree on the deadline and intermediate checkpoints.
4. **Set the right level of autonomy**
   - Use a "tell, show, do, review" gradient for newer folks.
   - For experienced folks, give the "what" and the "why," and let them choose the "how."

5. **Make a shared plan**
    - Ask them to restate the plan, risks, and first steps in their own words.
    - Confirm milestones, deliverables, and how progress will be reported.
6. **Provide resources and access**
    - Ensure that tools, information, budget, and introductions are in place.
    - Remove blockers early.
7. **Establish communication routines**
    - Agree on update cadence and format.
    - Define escalation triggers and how to reach you.
8. **Coach, don't micromanage**
    - Ask questions that guide thinking rather than take back the work.
    - Offer timely feedback focused on behavior and impact.
9. **Inspect what you expect**
    - Review against the agreed criteria at milestones.
    - Use samples or spot checks for quality without re-doing the work.
10. **Close the loop, and recognize**
    - Debrief: what worked, what to change next time.
    - Share credit publicly, and capture lessons learned.

Here's a template you can use to keep yourself on target.

- Outcome.
- Constraints and non-negotiables.
- Decision rights: You decide . . . , I decide. . . .

- Stakeholders and risks.
- Milestones and dates.
- Update cadence and format.
- Resources and access needed.

Of all the leadership traits in this book, delegating is more art than determination. Your experience as well as the seasoning of your team have a direct impact on what you delegate. What you delegate with one team might be something you have to hold with another. Delegation is a great practical exam as to how you are growing as a leader.

When it comes to leaders with impressive résumés, Moses is in the hall of fame. All Moses did was lead 600,000 men (possibly three million in total, including women and children) out of Egypt toward a promised land. Even with those credentials, he struggled with delegating. His father-in-law, Jethro, called him out in Exodus 18. Moses was mediating every small dispute among his fellow sojourners. He was unable or unwilling to say "No." In Exodus 18:17, Jethro said, "What you are doing is not good." He encouraged Moses to delegate. The wise advisor continued, "Look for able men from all the people, men who fear God, who are trustworthy and hate a bribe, and place such men over the people as chiefs of thousands, of hundreds, of fifties, and of tens. And let them judge the people at all times. Every great matter they shall bring to you, but any small matter they shall decide themselves. So, it will be easier for you, and they will bear the burden with you. If you do this, God will direct you, you will be able to endure, and all these people also will go to their place in peace." (Exodus 18:21–23).

Age and experience do not always bear fruit with wise delegation. David was the powerful king of Israel. His military victories were legendary, and his heart followed the Lord. Like all of us, David was broken, and his selfishness gave root to sin. 2 Samuel 11:1 says, "In the spring of the year, the time when kings go out to battle, David sent Joab, and his servants with him, and all Israel. And they ravaged the Ammonites and besieged Rabbah. But David remained at Jerusalem." David abdicated his responsibilities. This failure led to other sins, including adultery, lying, and murder. By failing to lead, David brought judgment down on himself, and the collateral damage affected his family and the nation of Israel for generations.

Abdicating is a trap that can easily entangle any of us. If you are blessed with a highly competent team, you can assume "they've got it." You may also be intimidated by their expertise and be fearful of having your inexperience exposed. A more insidious snare, but far more corrosive is the philosophy of "Do what only you can do." This phrase was made popular by the pastor of a large church. He said, "Leaders should focus on doing what only they can do, and delegate the rest." The words that come to mind when I read that statement include *absurd, selfish, arrogant, entitled, delusional* and *narcissistic.* These people are abdicators. Here's how they roll.

Abdication

- Vague ask: "Take care of this" with little context or criteria.
- No decision boundaries: the person has to guess what they own.
- No checkpoints: you disappear until the deadline.
- No support: missing access, introductions, or time to help.
- Surprise outcomes: you learn key facts only at the end.
- Blame or rework: you swoop in late, redo the work, or fault the person.
- BLUF. They care only about "their stuff" and how they look. They measure success in applauds and accolades.

It is vital that a leader has accountability in this area. You can't police yourself. You have to be confident enough to have contrarians in your life who will tell you the truth you don't want to hear. Don't seek fans to praise your selfless actions. Seek honest mirrors who will reflect reality.

Delegation is an intentional leadership act. A leader assigns clear outcomes, authority, and resources to someone else, while staying accountable for the result and providing coaching, guardrails, and check-ins. Abdication looks similar on the surface—work is handed off—but the leader disengages, withholds context, fails to set expectations, and distances themself from ownership when things get hard or interrupt their personal agenda. Delegation grows people and capacity, because responsibilities are matched to capability, support is present, and learning is captured. Abdication erodes trust and performance, because ambiguity rises, alignment falls, and accountability disappears. In short, delegation empowers without surrendering responsibility; abdication surrenders responsibility without empowering.

Application

Here's a quick self-audit to enable you to tell healthy delegation from abdication. Use a current task as your reference point. If you answer "No" to any Clarity, Authority, or Cadence questions, fix those before handing off. Write a one-page delegation brief: outcome, constraints, owners, milestones, risks, comms plan. Schedule the first checkpoint now, and ask for a written plan back within twenty-four to forty-eight hours.

Clarity of outcome

- Have I defined the desired result, success criteria, and deadline in writing?
- Does the person know what "done" looks like and what "not done" looks like?

Ownership and authority

- Have I assigned a single, accountable owner?
- Does this person have the authority, access, and resources to deliver without constant handoffs?

Why me? vs. Why them?

- Did I choose to delegate for development, bandwidth, or expertise reasons—not to avoid discomfort?
- Am I still accountable for the outcome, even though they own execution?

Scope and boundaries

- What decisions are theirs, which are mine, and where must we consult?
- What are the constraints they must respect: budget, risk, policy, quality bar?

Context and intent

- Have I shared the "why," stakeholders, and risks, so that they can make good trade-offs?
- Do they know how this work connects to larger goals?

Support and enablement

- Did I provide the starting materials, templates, examples, and contacts?

- Have I removed known blockers and secured cross-team dependencies?

Checkpoints and cadence

- Do we have a right-sized updated cadence, with dates and artifacts, not "ping me if needed"?
- Are there early milestones to surface drift before it's costly?

Communication quality

- Did I ask them to restate the plan in their own words to confirm alignment?
- Do we agree on how to raise risks quickly and how decisions will be documented?

Feedback and standards

- Have I defined quality standards with examples?
- Will I give timely, specific feedback on drafts without taking the work back?

Risk and escalation

- What are the top risks and pre-agreed-upon triggers for me to step in, pivot, or escalate?
- Is there a contingency if capacity, quality, or timing slips?

Development and growth

- Does this stretch their skills appropriately with support?
- Have we identified one skill they'll practice and how we'll review it?

Signals that you're delegating

- Clear outcome, owner, authority, and constraints
- Defined cadence and early checkpoints
- Support provided, risks named, feedback loop active

Signals that you're abdicating

- Vague ask, like "own this" without scope or success criteria
- No access, authority, or resources granted
- "Let me know if you need anything" instead of a cadence
- You disappear and then, later, criticize or reclaim the work

CHAPTER 11

★★★★★★★

Flexibility and Adaptability

Italian General Giulio Douhet is renowned for his theories on air power. His work in *The Command of the Air* is more than 100 years old but remains relevant today. A signature quote from Douhet is, "Flexibility is the key to airpower." He asserted that it is vital for aviation assets to be able to shift between missions, locations, and objectives. This ability to adapt made air power the most lethal force on the planet. This remains true today.

Air power as presented by the United States military has several aspects. All branches of the service have air assets. The Army, Navy, Marine Corps, and Coast Guard primarily support operations internal to their organization, while the Air Force and Space Force are utilized across the entire spectrum of operations. This breadth of aviation resources is further complemented by a vast array of weapon systems. Tanker aircraft make the United States' reach nearly unlimited. Transport planes provide strategic and tactical airlift of personnel and cargo anywhere in the world. These two platforms make it possible for fighter, attack, and bomber aircraft to "reach out and touch someone" anytime and anywhere. Even the division of forces from active-duty, to National Guard, to reservist provide the Department of War coverage through the routine and a shock absorber to handle when world events flex.

As a pilot, sitting alert is a practical way in which the Air Force demonstrates the flexibility of air power. There are several different postures of alert. Fighter aircraft sit alert at locations around the country as part of the Aerospace Control mission. When you think about airplanes responding to a threat, this is the image movies put in your mind. A plane is pre-flighted, fueled, and ready to launch. A pilot sits in a dormitory-type room only minutes away from the jet. A klaxon sounds, and everyone is sprinting to their assigned location. The pilot slips on his flight suit and runs to his plane like Superman coming out of a phone booth or Batman emerging from the Batcave. Within five minutes, a jet engine roars into the sky, bringing the sound of both hope and harm, depending on which end of the mission you are on.

Other aircraft maintain alert, but these weapon systems don't have the same public-relations agents as fighter pilots. Bombers, tankers, and airlifters have the same position of readiness. As an airlift pilot, I sat alert countless times. Sometimes we were notified and raced to the plane, only to be met on the ramp by an exercise inspector who just wanted to make sure we were ready. On some occasions, we received notification and didn't receive our final tasking until we were airborne. During other instances, I got a "preview of coming attractions" from a well-placed but unnamed source. One preview came on September 14, 1994.

The government of Haiti was overthrown in September 1991. Raoul Cedras led the uprising. The next several years saw a refugee crisis coined the "Haitian Boat People," and within eighteen months, thirty-eight thousand refugees were intercepted by the Organization of American States. International sanctions did nothing to bring the regime down. In September 1994, President Bill Clinton sent a diplomatic delegation led by former President Jimmy Carter and retired

General Colin Powell to negotiate a transition back to the freely elected president Jean-Bertrand Aristide. Negotiations were not progressing, so the United States decided to incentivize the proposal.

I was alerted from Charleston AFB, South Carolina, and told to fly to Pope AFB, North Carolina. Upon arrival, we began to load members of the 82nd Airborne Division with the Division Ready Force 1 (DRF-1). The ramp was full of airplanes and airborne troopers. We buttoned up the airplane, started the engines, and got ready for the three-hour flight to Haiti. The mission called for us to drop the troops and their equipment, which would signal the start of Operation Uphold Democracy. I called the air-traffic-control tower for clearance to taxi. I was told to hold and contact C2 (Command and Control). We maintained our position and hailed them on another radio. The C2 controller said, "Stand down. Mission terminated. Shut down. Deplane all personnel and cargo, and report to command post." I asked the controller to repeat his instructions and authenticate using the day's classified code word. He confirmed the transition, and we complied.

While standing in command post, the duty officer had no additional information. He relayed his orders. I went up the chain of command and contacted Military Airlift Command at Scott AFB, Illinois. The only additional information I received was to go to the base's billeting office, get a room, and go to bed; they would call in the morning. I assumed we were on a twenty-four-hour hold for some reason. I figured we'd get a call and execute the mission the next night. Additional clarity broke through the morning sky the next day when C2 called and informed me my mission was to take the aircraft back to Charleston. I mumbled something like "This is a cluster," showered, got dressed, went to the airplane, and flew back to Charleston.

When I landed in Charleston later in the day on September 15, I heard the rest of the story. Video of the activity on the ramp at

Pope AFB was sent to the Carter delegation. They told Cedras the video was a live-feed of the 82nd Airborne on their way to depose the current government and restore order. The Haitian leader had no idea the video was several hours old. Cedras relented. It took a few days to work out the details. On September 19, Operation Uphold Democracy did take place, but with a mostly peaceful landing and deployment of U.S. troops to restore order.

Leaders understand they need a tool belt full of skills. Experience teaches which traits to employ at the appropriate time, and wisdom whispers when to flex. This sound of a gentle breeze is the cue to adapt the plan. Fear, impatience, and recklessness are clanging cymbals. Flexibility is a quiet resolve that comes from beyond mental acuity and physical force. It is birthed in the deep recesses of contemplation and rehearsed in the space between soul and spirit.

Flexible leaders adapt to reality instead of forcing reality to fit a plan. That matters because:

- **Change is constant.** Markets, teams, and constraints shift. Flexibility lets you adjust quickly instead of getting stuck on outdated assumptions.
- **Better decisions under uncertainty.** When you can pivot, you can test, learn, and iterate rather than bet everything on one path.
- **Higher team trust and engagement.** People feel heard when leaders adjust to new information and diverse perspectives.
- **Resilience in crises.** Flexibility turns disruptions into options, reducing panic and enabling faster recovery.
- **The margin to re-sequence, reprioritize, or redefine "good enough" is a valuable tool.**

- **Innovation.** Openness to trying alternatives invites creativity and continuous improvement.

Flexibility can be practiced. Just like an athletic team divides their practice into segments such as stretching, drills, situational preparation, and positional focus, a leader can prepare. Elements of preparation include:

- **Hold principles tightly and plans loosely.**
- **Define goals in outcomes, not methods.**
- **Build short feedback loops, and pre-define pivot triggers.**
- **Encourage dissent and surface weak signals early.**
- **Retain optionality:** resource buffers, modular plans, and clear decision rights.
- **Reflect regularly:** What changed? What did we learn? What should we do now?

There are two danger signs on the road to becoming a flexible leader. Indecision and people-pleasing are traps that seek to entangle. How do you recognize when you are slipping toward these snares or have already been captured? The signs of an indecisive leader are:

- **Drifts on goals:** Priorities or success criteria keep shifting without a stated reason.
- **Perpetual reconsideration:** Decisions are reopened frequently with no new information.

- **Approval seeking:** Prolonged consensus-chasing that stalls action.
- **Avoids commitment:** Prefers more analysis over making a reversible call.
- **Vague rationale:** Can't explain why they changed course beyond "It felt right."
- **Missed timeboxes:** Deadlines slip with no explicit reset or plan.

Regarding people-pleasing, I'll expand on the areas of caution. My experience in the local church finds this trait more widespread and problematic. One or two of the signs below aren't definitive; look for patterns over time.

Behavioral signs

- Says "Yes" quickly, regrets it later, and then overextends or cancels
- Volunteers for low-value tasks to be seen as helpful, even when bandwidth is tight
- Avoids delivering bad news or tough feedback; uses softeners to the point of vagueness
- Changes stance, depending on who is in the room

Boundaries and priorities

- Struggles to set or hold boundaries, especially with senior or vocal peers
- Lets others' urgency override planned priorities repeatedly
- Rarely delegates, or takes work back to keep others happy

Decision patterns

- Defers decisions until there's broad approval, even for reversible calls
- Reopens settled choices at the first sign of discomfort from someone
- Frames choices in terms of keeping peace rather than achieving outcomes

Communication cues

- Excessive agreement language: "I'm good with whatever," "No worries at all," "It's totally fine," when it clearly isn't
- Hedging or self-erasing qualifiers: "This might be dumb, but . . ."
- Overexplains to justify harmless requests or reasonable "No's"

Emotional markers

- Visible anxiety when others are displeased or silent
- Takes critical feedback as personal rejection
- Relief when praised for being "nice," more than for impact

Relationship dynamics

- Over-identifies with being the "glue" or "go-to helper"
- Protects relationships at the expense of standards or commitments
- Avoids conflict, triangulates, or uses side channels instead of direct conversations

Impact on work

- Scope creep and missed deadlines due to over-commitment
- Quality slips from rushing to meet everyone's asks
- Burnout signs: cynicism, exhaustion, quiet resentment

Flexible, adaptable leaders read the context, adjust plans quickly, and keep teams moving when assumptions change. They treat new information as fuel, not a threat, revisiting goals and reallocating resources without losing sight of the mission. This creates psychological safety, because people see that learning and course-correction are expected. Adaptable leaders also widen their options by seeking diverse perspectives, running small experiments, and deciding based on evidence rather than ego. The result is resilience: faster recovery from setbacks, better use of opportunities, and sustained trust in the face of uncertainty.

Even with these compelling points, perseverance seems to be at odds with adaptability. Isn't the way to success paved with grinding it out, sticking to the plan, and never compromising? A look at God in this seeming paradox provides a handle to grasp.

Hebrews 13:8 says, "Jesus Christ is the same yesterday and today, and forever." In Malachi 3:6(a), God states, "For I, the LORD, do not change." These verses are often referenced to support what is called the Doctrine of Immutability. Theologian William Greenough Thayer Shedd defines the concept as "the unchangeableness of God's essence, attributes, purposes, and consciousness." God's character never changes, but God is dynamic in how He interacts with and reacts to nature. The creation of man, the fall of man through sin, sending Jesus as the propitiation for those sins, and Jesus's resurrection are evidence of God's willingness to respond to nature's condition: unchanging character; compassionate response to circumstances.

The core values of a leader are unchanging. Character is not flexible. Integrity, commitment, discipline, IRS, feedback, evaluation, dealing with failure, humility, action, courage, and delegation are constants. A leader's response to changing conditions affects methodology without altering his essence. Flexibility is how a leader of uncompromising virtue corrects a compromised plan.

Application

Answer the questions below. Ask three people for feedback: one close family member or personal friend, one co-worker who works with you closely, and one co-worker who is a contrarian. Compare the answers among the three. Define one pivot rule today: "If X happens, we will switch to Option B." Run a seven-day flexibility practice: one small experiment, one assumption checked, one alternative invited, and one rule simplified.

Mindset and intent

- Am I prioritizing the outcome and principles, or my preferred method?
- What would "success" look like if it didn't happen my way?

Assumptions and evidence

- What assumptions am I making right now?

- What new facts would change my approach, and do I have a way to notice them?

Options and creativity

- What are three other viable ways to reach the goal?
- What is a smaller, reversible step I could try to learn faster?

Listening and input

- Have I asked for perspectives from people closer to the problem?
- Can I state the strongest version of an alternative view fairly?

Decision rules

- Which parts are truly non-negotiable (values, safety, legal), and which are preferences?
- What criteria would justify a pivot *vs.* staying the course?

Timing and responsiveness

- When did I last update the plan based on new information?
- What indicators would tell me to adjust today rather than next week?

Experiments and learning

- What low-cost experiment can I run in the next twenty-four to forty-eight hours?
- How will I measure learning and decide the next move?

Collaboration and ownership

- Am I giving others autonomy in "how" while being clear on the "what" and "why"?
- Have I made it easy for teammates to propose changes and surface risks?

Emotional signals

- Do I feel defensive, impatient, or attached to being right?
- If I pause and breathe, does a more-flexible option become acceptable?

Friction and environment

- Is there a simple change to constraints, tools, or schedule that would unlock progress?
- What's one thing I can remove to reduce rigidity (a rule, meeting, or step)?

Under pressure

- When stakes rise, do I narrow options or widen them thoughtfully?
- Can I hold clear standards while adapting tactics?

CHAPTER 12

★★★★★★★

Feedback

I was passing through eighteen thousand feet, on my way to twenty-one thousand feet, as I was navigating to the military operating area (MOA) north of Williams Air Force Base, Arizona, just outside of Chandler a few miles southeast of Phoenix. An MOA is a defined piece of airspace set aside by the Federal Aviation Administration (FAA) for the purpose of military training. I was on one of my first flights as a student at the Air Force's Undergraduate Pilot Training (UPT). I was in the left seat of a T-37. The Cessna T-37—affectionately called the "Tweet"—was a twin-engine jet trainer the Air Force used for its initial phase of flight training. In the right seat was Captain Rob Rau. Rob was an instructor pilot and, more accurately, a first-assignment instructor pilot (FAIP). Rob had completed pilot training three years previously and was selected to stay at Williams AFB as an instructor pilot for his first flying assignment. Most people didn't want to be a FAIP. They wanted to spread their wings, literally and figuratively, in the operational Air Force and leave the training command behind. Yet, the people selected to be FAIPs were usually near the top of their graduating class. Rob fit this model as an excellent aviator and good instructor, and he was itching to leave the confines of the Air Training

Command (ATC) and venture into the world, saving it for the sake of democracy via an Air Force jet.

As I watched the altimeter indicate a continued climb to my assigned flight level, I felt a rap on my helmet. It wasn't severe enough to put me into concussion protocol, but it got my attention. Next, I heard the unmistakable sound of Captain Rau over the airplane's communication system: "What are you doing?"

At this point in my training and development as a pilot, I can honestly say I didn't have any idea what I was doing. I felt that if I got my boots on the correct feet, my flight suit on properly, with the patches in the right spot, connected the oxygen hose to my helmet and could close the canopy on the plane, I was winning. Clearly, I'm not going to involve my instructor pilot in my little drama of insecurity. So, I just made up some stuff and hoped he would buy it.

No sale.

Captain Rau took control of the airplane. Blistered my ears for a few minutes. Might have allowed his left hand to renew acquaintances with my helmet a couple of more times. Then, he gave me control of the plane again, and we continued the sortie and training. When we landed about an hour and fifteen minutes later, we sat and debriefed the entire mission. And, when I say *the entire mission*, I mean we reviewed *every moment* from the pre-flight briefing, to getting our equipment in life support, to riding in the van to the airplane, to the exterior pre-flight of the aircraft, to starting the engines, taxiing, takeoff, every portion of the flight, landing, getting out of the plane, the post-flight inspection, completing the maintenance forms, the return ride in the van, cleaning our equipment, and returning to the flight room. It was the colonoscopy of debriefs. Ultimately, all of this was a thorough form of feedback. Captain Rau prepared me for my next flight—and flights for years to come—by reviewing, in painstaking detail, every correct decision, misstep, and moment of indecision. He left no stone unturned and no word unsaid. Difficult, uncomfortable, encouraging, and inspiring—I clearly knew where I stood and what I needed to do to advance.

Feedback is the process by which the effect of an action is returned or "fed back" to inform and possibly alter the ensuing action. Feedback can come from many sources, including bosses, peers, and subordinates, and it can originate from other life forms and even inanimate objects. Say "Whatever" to your spouse, and you'll get some feedback. Play with your dog's food bowl, and you might get some feedback. Bump your arm against the rack in your oven when you're pulling out a hot dish, and you'll get some feedback and a reminder to be more cautious.

Feedback can also come in several flavors. There's verbal and nonverbal, formal and informal. Sometimes it's negative, and, on other occasions, it's positive. The sender and receiver are the two participants in feedback. Feedback is a key component in training, development, learning, growth in listening, and self-awareness. With these unequaled benefits at our disposal, we should establish some key components of feedback. Here are five important properties.

1. **Timeliness.** Timing isn't everything in a good feedback model, but it can set a favorable atmosphere or cause shutdown instantaneously. When we were building our home, I was deployed for most of it, and Jennabeth had boots on the ground. She consistently went to the construction site and provided feedback. Some of it was preventative (noticing an incorrect paint color in the can), and some of it was responsive (that door is not in the right place according to the plans). Give feedback when something can be changed. Feedback to the barber after the first few cuts is helpful. Telling them the haircut is bad at the end—with no opportunity for course correction—is called *complaining.* Just

like in any other important conversation, try to avoid engaging someone who is hungry, angry, or tired. My wife, Jenna, and I don't talk about the budget just before we go to bed, and she usually doesn't give me her opinion on my housekeeping duties before dinner.

As an examiner pilot, I would administer flight evaluations to other pilots. One type of evaluation was an Operational Mission Evaluation (OME). This is a multi-day and usually multi-country mission where I observe the pilot commanding the crew and completing the assigned mission. It's grueling physically as well as mentally. I'm watching everything the aircraft-commander candidate is doing and asking questions along the way to test their knowledge. Since this is conducted over multiple days, I would give a little feedback every day. Usually, I would relieve the examinee on the final flight segment, fly the aircraft myself, and put them in a relaxed position to receive the overall assessment and feedback. The extra energy necessary to fly that final portion would have created undue fatigue and affected their ability to receive the feedback. By being deliberate with respect to timing, you enhance the chance for positive results. While being patient is important, procrastinating and over-delaying is as bad as acting too quickly. Postponement to unreasonable lengths makes the experience stale, knowledge and recall spotty, and both the giver and receiver solidified in their version of the facts. In most cases, a delay beyond twenty-four hours threatens the shelf life of quality feedback.

2. **Thoroughness.** After an operation or exercise in the Air Force, we would engage in a "hot wash." This is an after-action debriefing where all the pertinent facts are reviewed. There's an agenda or checklist and a narrator or after-action officer who facilitates

the conversation. There's a recorder who takes notes. This system is in place to provide a level of thoroughness to ensure critical aspects of the mission are analyzed and given feedback. Whether the feedback is one-on-one or a group setting like a hot wash, it's important to have some kind of structure. Create an agenda or checklist, and establish a timeframe for start and finish. Be open to venturing off-script for a moment if you see value, but be rigorous at keeping the agreed-to duration. Whoever is talking the most thinks it's the most valuable moments of a lifetime, and whoever is listening the most wants the other person to stop talking. If you want to keep talking, go call your Mom—she would love to hear from you—but don't ruin feedback by overvaluing your voice.

3. **Alterations.** I recently received a pair of lululemon pants for a gift. They were a bit too long, and the store offered an alteration service. The sales associate made the appropriate alterations, and a few days later, I returned to pick up my perfectly adjusted pants. They are my favorite pair. If I happen to gain some weight and the waistband becomes too tight, lululemon couldn't alter the pants to fit me. I'd either have to go on a diet or buy pants with a larger waist. In a feedback session, it's beneficial to talk only about things that can be altered. Discussing things outside of the giver's or receiver's control leads nowhere and can hijack a degree of self-awareness and self-discovery by affixing responsibility elsewhere. When I was flying at Delta Airlines, I was doing an approach to Runway 4L at Newark Liberty International Airport. The skies were partly cloudy, and visibility was good, but the winds were a challenge on this March day. That time of year, the winds are usually from the west, averaging ten miles per hour. A ten-mph crosswind is a routine landing. Today, the

winds were twenty-five mph, gusting to thirty-five mph. The maximum crosswind component for the aircraft was thirty-one knots, so I was right on the verge of not being able to land. As we approached the final phase of landing, the controller called the winds at twenty-nine knots, so I proceeded to land. Let's just say the landing was a little rough. I was standing at the cockpit door to thank the passengers as they were deplaning, and a 70-plus-year-old female passenger said, "Did we land or get shot down?" I appreciated her feedback and wanted to blame the winds for my landing. But I couldn't change the wind. In the future, I could learn how to more smoothly transition the controls from the approach phase to the landing phase taking out the crosswind controls and a timelier power reduction. BLUF—bottom line up front—talk about what you can control, and skip the things outside of your purview.

4. **Next.** Former U.S. Army Medic and Purple Heart recipient C.J. Stewart is a force. C.J. is constant movement, thought, and speech. Yet, all of that activity has an intended purpose and destination. A gifted teacher and communicator, one powerful characteristic he employs in every individual or group encounter is the challenge "What are your next steps, based on what God has said to you?" Philippians 1:6 says God will "perfect" His work, indicating He's not finished, so we're not done. Feedback by its very definition is designed to modify or change. A great technique to help someone learn through feedback is *coaching them toward next* rather than controlling it. For example, I prefer to ask the individual, "What do you think your next step is?" rather than prescribe what I think their response should be. Directing the step limits perspective to my thoughts rather than their learning. It also promotes merely following orders rather than developing

independent thinking and ownership. Questions allow for further investigating options around their actions. For example, "If you did that, what actions might that precipitate, and what would be your subsequent response?" Getting to the second- and third-level effects will likely allow the individual to start at a better initial next step. When the "next" is agreed upon, clear, quantifiable measures and specific time frame for completion are vital. If there are multiple action steps, ask the person receiving the feedback to prioritize each.

5. **Follow-up.** I was instructing a student pilot in aerial refueling. Flying multiple airplanes in close proximity to one another deliberately seems an act of lunacy. Operational requirements sometimes demand inflight refueling from a tanker aircraft in order to extend the duration a plane can remain airborne and reach the intended target or destination. The refueling plane is slightly higher than the receiver aircraft, as the tanker's refueling boom (the hose the jet fuel is dispersed from) trails at the back of the plane. As the receiver closes inside 100 feet and is climbing to an altitude just below the tanker, the trailing edge of the wings of the higher aircraft produces a downwash, causing the receiver to become slightly unstable. This continues until you get inside fifty feet, at which point the downwash is behind the receiver's flight path.

   During this fifty-foot window of experiencing the downwash, the pilot in the receiver aircraft often overcontrols the aircraft. The buffeting and unpredictable movement of the plane in such close quarters of another aircraft heightens the nerves of the pilot and causes him to "stir the pot." He essentially takes the stick of the airplane and stirs it like a big spoon in a pot. The pilot is actually moving the stick faster than the flight controls can respond. This momentary lag between input on the stick and the movement of the flight surfaces creates uncertainty in the pilot, causing him to move them even faster and more briskly, further exacerbating the problem. As an instructor, you advise the student to "stop moving the stick," "stop stirring the pot," or "freeze your hands," but at three-hundred-plus mph, twenty-five thousand feet in the air, and another airplane taking up your entire windshield, it's hard. The pilot also has a death grip on the stick.

As a "next," I would tell the student I wanted them to use only their first two fingers and thumb until our next flight-training session. Hold your fork or spoon with your first two fingers and thumb. Drive the car with your first two fingers and thumb. Open the mail, pick up a box, push the lawnmower, operate the vacuum cleaner with your first two fingers and your thumb. By doing this, I would help the pilot transition to using only their first two fingers and their thumb on the stick. This would eliminate them grasping the stick with their entire hand with a death grip. Then, I would teach the student pilot to use "pressure" on the stick as opposed to pronounced "movements." Marginal pressure is enough to cause slight movement of the flight controls, which is sufficient to position the plane properly in light of the downwash's effects on the aircraft. The follow-up from the next homework assignment usually produced positive results and an aerial-refueling qualification for the pilot.

These five properties of feedback (Timeliness, Thoroughness, Alterations, Next, and Follow-Up) establish a solid context for the giver *and* the receiver. Each participant has their own set of responsibilities in the interaction. Many are imbedded in the properties and are relevant to both participants. Here are a few additions to your tool belt, depending on your seat.

Giver

1. **Be Specific.** If you're flying an approach in a crosswind, you need to move the stick or the yoke such that the ailerons (flight-control surface on the wing) are into the wind. So, if the wind is coming from the right, you fly with the right wing down or into the wind. The rudder controls the *yaw* of the aircraft—the movement across its vertical axis. The pilot cross-controls the plane by pressing the left rudder pedal. As you prepare for landing, you reduce power and continue to keep the crosswind controls in through the touchdown phase. Releasing the crosswind controls too early will cause the wing on the wind side to lift up and possibly drag the opposite wing down to the ground. When you're giving a pilot feedback about this type of landing, you have to be that specific. You cover every phase, every eventuality, and their performance. Avoid terms like "good," "well," or "poor," as they have no quantifiable value. If you say someone performed "better," tell them how they improved.

2. **Honest.** Feedback should be honest. It doesn't have to be brutally honest. You can be kind and give feedback. We're discussing performance and not a person, so check personality evaluations at the door. I also recommend trashing the "sandwich approach." You don't have to tell someone three things they did well so you can provide a point of corrective feedback. When I would debrief flight evaluations for pilots, I started reviewing their performance based on the timeline of the day. The timeline started during the mission brief. During one check-ride, the pilot failed to coordinate our range times properly, and, when we arrived at the range, the controllers would not let us enter the airspace. After holding for a few minutes and making some radio calls, we were able to

continue the mission. One of my first points of feedback was to tell the pilot that this failure delayed our range time, cost us valuable fuel, and put the rest of the mission behind. I didn't tell him that his uniform looked nice that day or that his haircut was particularly sharp just to soften him up for telling him about a mistake he made. Be honest. Be kind. Be clear.

3. **Openness.** On one particular mission, I administered three initial-qualification pilot evaluations. An "initial qual" pilot is someone who is brand new to the airplane. They've flown a handful of simulator flights and somewhere around five flights in the jet. Usually, these check rides are quite busy, as the young aviator "doesn't know what he doesn't know." As the evaluator, you feel like you're doing the work of two. You're reviewing the student's performance while trying to make sure he doesn't kill you and him. After this flight, I was debriefing with all three simultaneously. As I went through my notes, I had made an annotation about one flight maneuver and attributed it incorrectly to the wrong pilot. As I was discussing the corrective action, the pilot sheepishly said, "Sir, that wasn't me. That was Lumpy." (Lumpy was the call sign of one of the other students). Embarrassed, I thanked him for the "feedback," and moved on to Lumpy. Even as the giver, you need to be open to feedback. Just because you're driving, it doesn't mean you're right. Be humble enough to be corrected.

Receiver

I break the receiver's duties down in the form of the stages of a pilot's mission.

1. **Mission Planning/Preflight.** What is your intended destination or mission? How will you navigate to that location? What

obstacles or threats do you face? Are there mechanical issues associated with the airplane that will impact your plan? These questions can be applied to a feedback conversation. The receiver, whether it's you or the person you're delivering the feedback to, has strengths, weaknesses, tendencies, and tells. Acknowledge these in advance, and let them inform you.

2. **Takeoff.** Takeoff and landing are the most dangerous stages of flight. This is because of space and time. Regarding space, you are closest to the ground during these times, and mistakes are more pronounced. With respect to time, because of the proximity to the ground, you have little time to recover from a mistake or manage an emergency with the unforgiving ground only feet away from a fast-moving aircraft. Compounding both of these variables is the increased workload during these transitional times of flight. Recognize that how you start is important. Are you nervous, defensive, unusually quiet, or unusually talkative? What is the environment telling you, and what is the tone of the giver? Don't allow those aspects to unduly influence your emotions.
3. **Cruise.** During cruise, it is easy to be complacent. You're thinking about the approach, landing, and mission, and you can minimize the importance of always being alert and prepared. Remain engaged throughout the conversation. The deliverer is setting the groundwork for the rating, score, assessment, or other metric, so pay attention to their words. These have to be a clear road map to next steps.
4. **Approach and Landing.** When the feedback plane is brought in for a landing, there shouldn't be any surprises. The deliverer should have laid out all aspects in a clear manner. If they didn't, it's time to ask questions—such as, "I understood you to say,

'_____.'" or, "As you were describing this area of performance, you noted that improvement was needed, but I don't understand how I get there." Avoid the tendency to express your frustration in "he said/she said" rebuttal. Relay your opinion in facts, rather than feelings. "I don't agree, because of 'x, y and z,'" as opposed to citing "fairness."

In addition to knowing these priorities, understanding the differences among self-awareness, self-analysis, and self-discipline is key to growth in receiving and acting upon feedback.

Self-awareness is noticing what's true in the moment about your inner and outer state.

It is the real-time perception of emotions, thoughts, body cues, motives, values, and how you're impacting others. Examples of awareness might be, "I'm getting defensive right now." "My energy dips after 3 p.m." There can be a risk if you overuse these kinds of negative "insight." Insight without change can drift into self-preoccupation.

Self-analysis is making sense of yourself over time. Reflective sense-making of patterns, causes, and options is the baseline. "Why is this happening?" and "What does it mean?"

Reflective techniques such as journaling, hypothesis-testing, and connecting dots across situations are helpful. A leader must guard against rumination and "paralysis by analysis." Elegant explanations and little movement are warning signs.

Self-discipline is doing what aligns with your values and goals, consistently. It follows a pattern of planning, committing, and following through, especially when it's hard. Routines, boundaries, accountability, and choosing long-term over short-term perspectives are the fuel that drives the self-discipline engine. Rigidness and ignoring feedback from feelings or context exemplify a person who lacks self-discipline.

Application

Solidifying the five priorities of feedback (Timeliness, Thoroughness, Alterations, Next, Follow-Up) in your interactions is the foundation. Next, recognizing, understanding, and addressing how self-awareness, self-analysis, and self-discipline show up or are absent in your life will provide finish and polish.

For additional help with the journey through the "self" triangle, review the statements below.

How do they work together?

- Order of operations: Awareness → Analysis → Discipline → Renewed Awareness.
- Feedback loop: Awareness supplies data. Analysis turns data into strategy. Discipline runs the strategy. Outcomes feed back into awareness to refine.

Quick practices

- Build self-awareness: Name emotions in real time. Set three to five daily "check-in" alarms to note mood, focus, and energy.
- Improve self-analysis: Weekly review with two prompts: "What patterns did I notice?" and "What one small change could test my hypothesis?"
- Strengthen self-discipline: Make it easy to start. Define the next visible action, tie it to a time and place, and track streaks. Use "commitment devices" like calendar blocks or a public promise.

A simple rule of thumb

- If you don't notice it, you can't analyze it.
- If you don't understand it, you'll misdirect your effort.
- If you don't act on it, nothing changes.

CHAPTER 13

★ ★ ★ ★ ★ ★ ★

Evaluation

Frank Howard had a legendary baseball career. A mountain of a man, Howard was known for his instant offensive production. In his time, there was not a power hitter more feared than Frank Howard. Defensively, he possessed an average arm and had fair speed for a man of his size. Following his playing career, he had several stints in coaching circles. Sometimes he coached from the bench, and, other times, he manned the first- or third-base coaching box. After a few years as an assistant coach, Frank took the helm of his own team as manager. I had the chance to play for Coach Howard during one of those stints.

Frank was not a man with an extensive vocabulary. Despite limited use of the spoken word, he had a way of communicating that was all his own. It sounded more like grunts and groans. Occasionally, these vocal emissions would transition into something like "geeeze" or "gooooosh." He did have one staple sentence. There was one series of words that signaled his complete frustration if they were directed to you. I was offered this evaluation on a few occasions. "Good gosh, Wiggins. That stinks," said Coach Howard.

Outside of a spanking or stern talking-to from my parents, this was one of my first opportunities to have a performance review. I suppose it worked. I had one of my best years in baseball as an All-Star selection as a catcher. Several of my teammates had banner years as well, which resulted in our team, the Yankees, winning the championship. Much of the credit goes to Frank Howard and his often-indistinguishable vocabulary assessing my performance.

For baseball fans out there, you may recognize the name Frank Howard. The fifteen-year major-league baseball veteran with four teams and a coach and manager for nine teams and twenty-two seasons had a sterling career in baseball. Yet, in all of his highlights, Howard was a coach for the Yankees, but never the manager, as I referenced above. That's fine, because, I never played for the New York Yankees or that Frank Howard. I played for the East Point, Georgia, Yankees and the Frank Howard who coached little-league baseball for this team of eleven- and twelve-year-old boys. The Frank Howard who had a son named Greg, who shared the diamond with me and about a dozen other knuckleheaded kids in the summer of 1973. I played for the Frank Howard who would bellow from the dugout for us to "get it in gear." That's the Frank Howard who was an early professor in my education on evaluation.

The terms "coaching," "feedback," and "evaluation" are all important facets in the growth and maturation of a child, athlete, employee, process, or organization. Ken Blanchard says that it's "the breakfast of champions." Writer Elbert Hubbard says that, if you want to avoid criticism and critique, "do nothing, say nothing, and be nothing." I want to be a part of something that makes an impact, whether that's a winning baseball team, an outstanding military unit, or a life-changing church.

When I joined the Air Force in 1987, the mission was to fly, fight, and win. This singular call shaped everything we did. It didn't matter how you felt about it or whether you had a head cold. It didn't matter if you liked your boss, had an argument with a friend, or were not selected for a job or promotion. All of that got checked at the door in order to have a laser focus on protecting our nation. From my first moments of basic training, where the way I stood, spoke, and looked were critiqued, to my retirement ceremony, there was constant evaluation. This mindset of continual review is a vital part of an always-improving military unit. We were able to be a part of a winning culture and specific winning teams directly due to our willingness to seek improvement.

The Air Force Outstanding Unit Award is presented by the Secretary of the Air Force to "units that have distinguished themselves by exceptionally meritorious service or outstanding achievement that clearly sets the unit above and apart from similar units. The services include: performance of exceptionally meritorious service, accomplishment of a specific outstanding achievement of national or international significance, combat operations against an armed enemy of the United States, or military operations involving conflict with or exposure to hostile actions by an opposing foreign force." I was a part of seven units that received this distinction. Basically, I was on the championship-winning team for seven of my twenty-five years assigned to eligible units. The members of these units expressed an overwhelming desire to improve through receiving analysis and appraisal. There were three common factors in these championship teams and their passionate desire to improve.

The Leader

It's important to have a capable leader who oversees the organization. Notice I did not say an *outstanding* leader. I didn't mention the need to be charismatic, a great communicator, or someone everyone praises as exhibiting great leadership ability (I'll discuss what defines and does not define leaders and leadership in another chapter). They simply need to be competent to do the job. Richard Hackman, former Harvard University social and organizational psychologist, highlighted four qualities that distinguished these kinds of leaders.

1. **Effective leaders know some things.** The leader should be an expert at some things and knowledgeable enough at others to understand how it affects the team and organization. There's a popular phrase that runs through leadership circles these days that leaders "should do what only they can do." That's a cute saying and completely wrong. A leader needs to be able to do whatever it takes to accomplish the vision and mission. You can't abdicate leadership because you don't know how to do something or hire around your personal desires because you don't like to do something, or because it "doesn't give you life." If that's your attitude, be a consultant and leave leadership to the professionals.
2. **Effective leaders know how to do some things.** Charles "Bud" Jackson was the commander of the 23rd Tactical Air Support Squadron (TASS) when I arrived in the unit in 1987. Lt. Col. Jackson was a veteran combat pilot, having flown F-105 Thunderchiefs in Vietnam and was currently leading a unit of OA-37 and OA-10 aircraft. The reason Jackson was the squadron commander was his past performance and future potential as an officer and aviator. Lt. Col. Jackson might not have been the "best stick" in the unit, but he was certainly one of the best. His flight evaluations were excellent, and his skill on the range in weapons delivery was commendable. He knew how to do the things that made a good fighter pilot. He was also a good instructor as he developed the Lieutenants and Captains under his charge. He wasn't an expert at supply and finance, but he knew enough to properly oversee his organization. The leader has to know how

to do some things and, principally, the things that are key to the organizational mission.

3. **Effective leaders should be emotionally mature.** Have you ever worked for a leader who was insecure? Ever been on a team whose leader tried to be just a regular guy too much? Have you seen leaders who want to power up on everyone, belittle people, or who fear making decisions? All of these characteristics stem from someone who is not emotionally mature. In Patrick Lencioni's book *The Ideal Team Player*, the author describes three characteristics that make a great teammate as being someone who is hungry, humble, and smart. They also describe an effective leader. Qualities like being hungry and humble indicate emotional maturity.

4. **Effective leaders need a measure of personal courage.** To push a team forward, the leader must disrupt its routines and challenge its definition of what is normal or acceptable. Since this often generates resistance and even anger, leaders must have the courage to stand apart. Courage has three elements. First, courage has a source. You must be confident with your identity as the source of your courage. Identity that comes from pleasing others, attaining wealth and titles, being feared, or acting from fear are parts of a false identity. As a man of faith, I often say identity is knowing who you are and whose you are. My identity is rooted in what God says about me. He says that I'm created in His image (Genesis 1:27), a new creation (2 Corinthians 5:17), His workmanship (Ephesians 2:10), fearfully and wonderfully made (Psalm 139:14), and that I am chosen (Ephesians 1:4). Next, courage requires a proper pace that is equal measures of patience and prudence. The prophet Samuel told David he would become king of Israel in 1 Samuel 16:13, but it wasn't until 2 Samuel 5, some fifteen years later, that he took the throne. Conversely,

Mordecai tells Esther in Esther 4:14 that now is the time to act. You have to take the right course as you act courageously. Finally, courage has a foundation of preparation that fuels the force of action. When I experienced a catastrophic engine failure immediately after takeoff from Goose Bay, Canada, the successful emergency landing we executed was the result of fifteen years of preparation in the classroom and simulator, and thousands of hours of experience in the airplane. The force of courage is grounded in preparation that fuels action.

Followers who are owners

As a part of the leadership at the Air Force Officer Training School (OTS), we had an honor code that stated, "We will not lie, steal, or cheat, nor tolerate among us anyone who does." The difference between being an employee and being an owner in an organization is the last portion of this code. Employees might uphold standards and work so as to accomplish the vision and mission of the company. But owners do their part, laterally assist others, and demand excellence. Joe O'Toole was the athletic trainer for the Atlanta Hawks from 1969 to 1997. I worked with Joe from 1984 to 1987. While his title was athletic trainer, Joe was also chief of logistics, part-time therapist, and head of analytics. Joe had so many jobs that the sign to his office read, "Hey, Joe," because everyone called Joe about everything. Ted Turner might have owned the Hawks, Stan Kasten may have been the general manager, and Bob Wolfe may have had the moniker of business manager, but Joe O'Toole was an owner in his actions, because there wasn't a job too big or too small for him. If you hear someone say, "That's not in my job description," that person might as well say, "I'm only here to rent from this organization." On the other hand, when someone steps out of their role and asks, "How can I help?" they are showing signs of putting the vision, mission, and team ahead of themselves.

I was the squadron commander of the 183rd Airlift Squadron for more than three years. The unit was composed of pilots, loadmasters, life-support technicians, and administrators who flew and supported the Mississippi Air National Guard's C-17 aircraft. This tactical and strategic airlift plane is the military's workhorse when it comes to aviation movement. Part of my duties entailed hiring future pilots for the organization. When I took the helm as the commander, the traditional hiring methodology was for the commander to lead the process and occasionally take input from the number-two in command, the Director of Operations (DO). While having the authority to make these critical manning decisions is powerful, I didn't believe building the organization in this manner was wise. I instituted a new hiring process, starting with naming a board president that was a Major. This is someone who is in an early leadership position and is a promotion away from being a DO or commander. Next, I added a senior enlisted member to the team—usually a loadmaster. This addition would provide needed perspective from the enlisted corps and help the officer-heavy board avoid blind spots. The remaining three to four board members were Captains and Lieutenants. These board members would be the peers of the future pilot. This gave added insight to the group looking for potential in the applicant with respect to character and competency to be a part of our unit.

The shift in the makeup of the board was very successful. The statistics to prove it included a higher graduation rate at flight school as well as a higher retention rate after the initial commitment to the military expired. These board members were not just employees or just military-service members; they were owners in the vision and mission of our unit.

The System

In order to create a culture of successful evaluation, you must have a system that supports it. The Hawk-Eye tennis-officiating system is an electronic line judge designed to call balls in or out in a tennis match. Outside of a programming error or an environmental anomaly, it has proven accurate to 3.6 millimeters. The system was introduced to minimize error and provide a more level field in judging the line calls of this sport. When it comes to a rating-and-review process, humans are at the helm, so there is a subjective nature to all systems; however, finding or developing a process that minimizes subjectivity is key. Two Air Force evaluation systems show the contrast between effective and ineffective review.

The Officer Performance Report (OPR) is given to every officer regardless of his job. Its checks-and-balances, simplicity, and narrative form give the appearance of minimizing subjectivity and concentrating on the officer's actual performance. Yet, reality says that more than 90 percent of OPRs are positive, and additional raters and reviewers concur with comments at the same rate. The subtle differences in OPRs are the unwritten code in the language. If someone completed a task or mission in an "outstanding" manner, that superlative carries more weight than accomplishing something with "excellence." If the act was completed "satisfactorily," that is tantamount to "unacceptable." In my experience, the difference between the OPR of a "marginally performing" and "exceptional" officer is negligible. This turns the review system into an exercise of documentation but not a reasonable review of performance.

On the other hand, the evaluation process for a *pilot* is filled with standards and measurables. Check rides, as they are called, are completed on an Air Force Form 8. One portion of the evaluation tests the pilot's knowledge of emergency procedures. Often called

"Boldface" for the type of print used to annotate these items in the aircraft technical manual, a pilot must know these procedures by heart and without error. It doesn't matter how the evaluator feels or whether the test subject is likeable. You either know it or don't; pass or fail. There's also a written and oral examination portion to be completed. While there is some latitude in completion percentage, there are right and wrong answers for operating limits of the aircraft, to rules of flight, to checklist procedures.

The final portion of the evaluation is the flight practicum. As with the previous portions of this review, there are standards for completion. Maneuvers must be completed within airspeed limits of +/- five knots or altitude limitations of +/-fifty feet. Landings have to be made in the prescribed landing zone and timing to arrive at military operating areas (MOA) to conduct ordnance delivery or drop zones is +/- 1 minute. All of these defined markers minimize the subjectivity of the evaluation and highlight actual performance against a set of agreed-upon standards.

How do you know if you're growing, improving, and developing without goals and a way of measuring your progress to the goals? As Christians, we applaud effort. This isn't true in other aspects of our lives, so why should it be true for the most important thing we do . . . following Jesus? Peter Drucker said, "If you can't measure it, you can't improve it." I would add that if you don't measure it, you don't care about it. What are some markers by which you can gauge your growth?

1. **Outcome/Results.** This is the numbers portion. There's a book in the Bible called Numbers. Jesus fed five thousand. Gideon counted his troops. In the Book of Acts, a story is recounted where three thousand people were baptized and added to the rolls. Numbers matter, and we should track them, because behind every number

is a person, a story, and a next step. How many times did you share the story of Jesus this week? How many days do you read your Bible? How often do you pray? The goal isn't the number. The number is an indication that you place value in the area.

2. **Stories.** I love a good story. Stories are the main course of the meal, while the numbers are the sides. Sharing and celebrating someone's salvation, obedience in baptism, giving, going, serving is a Jesus Pep Rally. Do you have any stories to share of God doing life-changing things in and through you?

3. **Strategy.** Michael Porter says, "Sound strategy starts with having the right goal." It's impossible to evaluate your growth as a disciple of Jesus unless you have a strategy. Strategy ensures you're asking the right questions about goals and objectives. Are you pointed in the right direction to accomplish what you've set your mind and heart toward?

4. **Season of Life.** Many variables have an influence on your season. If you're a full-time student, that's a season. If you're a parent of small children, that's a season. If you're receiving mail from AARP, that's a season. Seasons don't determine *if*; they only determine *when*. Seasons speak to when and how. When Jesus said, "Go therefore" in Matthew 28, he didn't qualify or disqualify anyone. The commission is for all. Don't let your season dictate if you step into your identity. Let it inform how, where, and when you act.

5. **Development.** Ephesians 4:11–13 says, "And He gave some as apostles, and some as prophets, and some as evangelists, and some as pastors and teachers, for the equipping of the saints for the work of service, to the building up of the body of Christ; until we all attain to the unity of the faith, and of the knowledge of the Son of God, to a mature man, to the measure of the stature

which belongs to the fullness of Christ." We are called to develop the gifts we are given. To do this, you must grow as Jesus grew. Luke 2:52 gives us the blueprint: "And Jesus kept increasing in wisdom and stature, and in favor with God and people." You need a growth-and-development plan that has those four elements—of growing in wisdom, stature (physically), favor with God, and favor with man. So, what's your plan? Here's mine:

- **Wisdom (Mind)**
  - Read twenty-four books (in genres of leadership, emotional health, military, biographies)
- **Personal growth.** Weekly counseling and/or life coaching
- **Professional growth.** Podcasts, network
- **Stature (Body)**
  - Daily walks and afternoons with Peloton
  - Daily vegetables and fruit
  - Average six hours of sleep daily. If I'm averaging only four at night, figure out how to nap.
- **Favor with God**
  - Daily Bible-reading plan
  - Actively attend and serve in a local church
  - Sabbath . . . *without excuse*
  - Daily meditation, contemplation, listening (*Lectio Divina* daily)
  - Scripture memorization. As Holy Spirit impresses the verse or chapter on me, add it to my immediate recall.
- **Favor with Man**
  - Continue in Men's Small Group

- Volunteer in a community activity or non-profit
- Invest in others through marriage mentoring or personal coaching

6. **Attitude (Alignment and Attunement).** Author Roger Harrison defines "alignment" as a "shared understanding and acceptance of an organization's purpose." Vision serves as the compass's north, directing efforts. Proper alignment brings great commitment and dedication. While *alignment* is the "service of will," *attunement* is the "service of love." Here, love is the "strong feelings of affection and positive value which people experience toward work that they do." It's the community aspect or a sense of camaraderie. Think harmony and unity. For evaluation purposes, are you in alignment and attunement with your family and friends regarding the priority of your spiritual growth? Faithful and fruitful, purposeful and passionate, committed and completed? In land navigation, you have to constantly re-orient yourself to a known landmark in order to ensure you're advancing properly. Observe your track to evaluate if you're maintaining course.

7. **Values.** In the cockpit of an airplane, there are numerous instruments that display the status of the operating systems. The pilot can see oil and hydraulic pressure, engine RPMs and temperatures, fuel quantities, navigation progress, and more. Values are the instrumentation of your organization. They help you monitor health and serve as a rally station and reminder of who you are and how you agree to work and live in order to accomplish your mission. Evaluating performance against values ensures you're doing it the right way.

8. **Evaluation.** Legendary basketball coach John Wooden said, "Without proper evaluation, failure is inevitable." While we

know we will fail because we're human and sinful, our failures might be limited to "how" we did something rather than "what" or "why" we did it if we employ a system of evaluation. If the thought of evaluation makes you uneasy, then, it's likely you value comfort more than change, critique, and correction. Stagnation and satisfaction are enemies of a spiritual movement. 2 Kings 7 tells the story of four men with leprosy sitting outside the gate of Samaria. The city was under siege by the Arameans, and famine had descended on the residents. The men knew that they would die from starvation if they remained where they were. If they attempted to enter the camp of the raiding Arameans, they would likely be killed. The four decided they would go to the camp. In the story's conclusion, God caused the Arameans to hear the sound of a great army, and they fled their camp. The four men entered the empty camp, finding food as well as silver, gold, and clothes. They returned to Samaria and told the residents of their findings, helping save the city.

Are you hungry enough to rise from your seat of comfort, venture toward the unknown that evaluation offers, and explore the opportunity that change and growth offer? If so, the evaluation starts with you.

Application

An effective evaluation system starts with having the right leader for the right follower in the right system. While the system must have standardization, the leader and the follower didn't roll off an assembly line. This is an area where the military-leadership model is challenged to translate to the civilian community and the church. All Air Force pilots go through the exact same curriculum. While the instructors and evaluators have different personalities, the methods, techniques, and procedures are identical.

The same can't be said for leaders in the church. I can't expect standardized performance when "they didn't grow up in my house or under my rules." What does translate to the faith community are the key elements of a thorough evaluation system. Ensure that your process employs Outcome/Results, Stories, Strategy, Season of Life, Development, Attitude, and Values.

Outcomes/Results

- What outcomes/results were delivered, and how do they compare to goals and objectives?
- Which of these results have the biggest impact?
- Which outcomes did not meet expectations? What is the concrete plan to meet them in the future?

Stories

- What story/stories from your area are reasons to celebrate?
- What story/stories reveal areas of opportunity or improvement?
- What story do you hope to hear next year, and what is your role in fostering it?

Strategy

- How was your strategy to reach your outcomes/results effective?
- How was your strategy to reach your outcomes/results ineffective?
- What will you change and keep the same regarding strategy for the future?

Season of Life (The leader's assessment of the team member)

- Does the team member's current life commitments and constraints allow them to focus on their role to the degree it requires to be successful? Consider family, caregiving, health, finances, and bandwidth for travel or hours.
- Does the team member have a support system in place to handle the rigors of the role? This includes teammates, volunteers, family, friends, and you (their leader).
- Does the team member desire to be in the role, or is it a step required for their desired position? Were they reassigned due to incompatibility with another position?

Development

- As stated above, use outline in Luke 2:52 as the standard.

Attitude (The leader's assessment of the team member)

- When faced with adversity, how did the team member respond?
- When work is ambiguous or unglamorous, do they act on it with the same enthusiasm as when the work is noticeable and public?
- Do they share credit, help others outside of their job duties, and engage in self-improvement?

Values

- Does the team member exemplify the values prescribed to the staff? Be specific with examples. Fight generalizations. If you are unsure, this indicates a problem for both the leader and the team member.

CHAPTER 14

★★★★★★★

The Battle Plan

Part One

I was sitting in the cockpit of an Air Force C-141 in July at Charleston Air Force Base, South Carolina. It was hot. As Eugene Morris, the character played by Matthew Broderick in the movie *Biloxi Blues* would say, "Boy, it's hot. This is hot. It never got this hot in Brooklyn. This is like Africa hot. Tarzan couldn't take this kind of hot." My flight suit appeared as if I had run through a sprinkler. My copilot, call sign "SLAP," which is an acronym for Sweats Like a Pig, was, well, living up to his name. We were conducting the aircraft preflight when we found a problem.

The C-141 had 6 radios. It had 2 Very High Frequency (VHF) radios for communicating with the air-traffic-control system. It had 2 Ultra High Frequency (UHF) radios for communicating with military command-and-control facilities. High Frequency (HF) radios are for communicating with users at long distances, sometimes as far as 1,900 miles. We were testing the 2 HF radios, and they were not working.

Today's mission had us flying from Charleston to Rota Naval Air Station, Spain. Since we would be crossing the Atlantic Ocean, we would need the HF radios. When crossing the ocean, you are not visible to land-based radar. In order to ensure separation from other planes, you begin to communicate with Oceanic Control. When crossing the Atlantic Ocean, you're flying on the North Atlantic Tracks (NATs). These are virtual highways in the sky. They are designated by letters such as "NAT A" and are defined by latitude and longitude—like 56 degrees North/50 degrees West, 55 degrees North/40 degrees West, 55 degrees North/30 degrees West, and so forth. Navigation procedures require you to contact the agency with oversight for their portion of the ocean and report when you arrive at a specific point, such as 55 North and 30 West—what time you arrived, your altitude, your next point on the route, such as 55 North and 20 West, estimated time at that point and the ensuing point thereafter. All of this word salad allows someone to track your progress and be alert to any conflicts, since there is no radar to provide separation of aircraft. Because the distance to the reporting stations in places such as Gander, Newfoundland, Canada, or Shanwick, in the Republic of Ireland, is so vast, an HF radio is your only means of communication.

I called maintenance and reported the problem. The readiness of an airplane is described as its "Alpha Status." Alpha One means the airplane is ready to fly, with no maintenance issues that would detract from its capability to complete the mission. Alpha Two indicates some minor discrepancies that should not impact the mission. Alpha Three means the plane is broken and not capable of flying the prescribed mission. The HF radios had to be operational to cross the ocean, so we were Alpha Three. The mission wasn't going anywhere until the problem was fixed. This meant the equipment and personnel the U.S. Navy had on the plane were going to be delayed.

I wrote the equipment malfunction in the aircraft's maintenance log. This book contains the history of the plane's discrepancies. I simply wrote, "HF radios inoperable."

When you report a plane as Alpha Three, you get lots of attention. Everyone wants an on-time departure. So, not only did the maintenance technician show up at the plane, but his supervisor was in tow. Additionally, the maintenance chief and duty officer showed up in a spotless Air Force truck. These two guys supervise the maintenance shift. They sit in an air-conditioned office and listen for problems on the radio. They try to alleviate the issues with radio calls, but occasionally, they are required to leave their 72-degree, climate-controlled office, brave the elements, and venture onto the flight line. I was concerned the heat might make them sweat. That would be tragic.

After several minutes of checking and testing the radios, the young Senior Airman, approximately twenty years old, said to me, the aircraft and mission commander, a Captain in the United States Air Force, that we were "good to go." I asked about the nature of the problem, just in case it recurred while we were away. His insight could help us troubleshoot more precisely and efficiently. The Senior Airman pointed me to the maintenance log.

He wrote, "The HF radio does not work in the OFF mode." There was nothing wrong with the radio. It didn't work because I didn't turn it on.

Things don't work if you don't turn them on. That's true for radios. It's also true for ovens, hair dryers, cars, computers, lamps, and cell phones. You have to turn them on to activate their resource and thus their usefulness. With leadership, you have to learn how to turn it on.

For nearly thirty years, I learned and practiced leadership as a member of the United States Air Force. From my first minutes at Officer Training School (OTS) as a trainee through my retirement ceremony, leading has been part of my job as a serviceman, as well as my passion. As a trainee and a newly minted 2nd Lieutenant, I was primarily taught about leading myself. Next, I advanced to leading others in the form of an aircrew or an organizational section called a "flight," consisting of ten to thirty personnel. As I further progressed, I commanded a squadron (a few hundred individuals), a group (several squadrons), and finally a wing (several groups). Along the way, there were deliberate and systematic steps the Air Force and my specific commanders took to educate me about leadership. There were formal courses to attend at each interval of promotion. There were annual performance reviews focusing primarily on your actions as an officer. There were technical evaluations of my ability as a pilot. Even after every flight and mission, the crew debriefs the events to capitalize on best practices and bring attention to areas needing improvement. In other words, leadership was taught, caught, and sought.

When I retired from the Air Force in 2013, I accepted a position working at the church my wife, Jennabeth, and I were attending. The church was a multi-site model, with five geographically separated locations around the state and a combined weekly attendance in excess of 12,000. My role entailed serving as a pastor to the church's 175-person staff as well as their families. Additionally, I was charged with working with our team to design and deliver resources for the purpose of educating and training our staff in the areas of professional- and personal-leadership development. My "additional duties as assigned" included heading up our residency and internship programs as well as spearheading our recruiting, interviewing, and hiring functions. Combining my experience in the leadership realm in the context of faith and the church seemed too good to be true.

Upon arriving on staff at the church, I noticed something troubling. Lynn Cole, a retired Air Force Colonel, is famous for saying, "Sometimes you have to call the ugly baby, an ugly baby." It was Lynn's homespun way of saying you need to be honest, and sometimes brutally honest. The Bible modifies Colonel Cole's quote, calling men and women of faith to "speak the truth in love" in Ephesians 4:15.

So, here's the truth in love: most of the staff who oversee the local church and the volunteers they produce are untrained and unprepared in the art of leadership. They have never been properly taught and trained. Most assume that, because they've been hired into or given a job title, leadership talent just miraculously descends upon them. It doesn't. Most have no accountability or effective feedback mechanism. Even if they do, the person providing the feedback is just as inept at leadership as they are. Leadership requires diligent learning, thoughtful practice, and continual growth. That's the ugly baby.

Despite years of allowing our eyes and ears to be tickled by poor substitutions, we can take and secure the battle space that is leadership through education, experience, and endurance, all wrapped in excellence. In the Air Force, we called it an Air Tasking Order (ATO). Other services describe a Commander's Intent. Regardless of nomenclature, this battle plan has a three-phase approach.

Phase 1 (Basic Training)

The Bible outlines a baseline of leadership qualifications. 1 Timothy 3, Hebrews 13, and 1 Peter 5 paint a clear picture of what Leadership 101 is. These attributes include:

- Temperate, prudent, respectable, hospitable, able to teach, not addicted to wine, not pugnacious, gentle, peaceable, not in love with money
- Faithful to his wife, manages his own family well, has children who are respectful and obedient
- Diligent, accountable, beyond reproach, humble, selfless, servant, integrity, honest, faithful

Let me reiterate. These are the minimum standards. It's freshman math, science, and humanities. This is what gets someone through the AI filter of basic qualifications. These characteristics allow for consideration. In order to proceed, you have to volunteer, attend, and complete Leadership Candidate School.

Phase 2 (Leadership Candidate School)

Someone aspiring to leadership doesn't master the prerequisites of Basic Training, but they do live a life consistently adhering to these qualities. When this is the pattern of their life, their next step is being a leadership candidate. The leadership qualities previously outlined in this book provide the curriculum, coupled with the practicum for phase two. Throughout the gospels, Jesus's actions give credence to and practical examples of these edicts. These examples are not exhaustive, but they do provide a clear correlation between the leadership quality and Jesus's actions that endorse and represent each.

- **Integrity/Honor.** In Matthew 25, Jesus mentions the hungry, thirsty, strangers, naked, sick, and prisoners. By calling us to care for people in various states of need, Jesus calls us to honor them.
- **Commitment.** In the gospel of John, there is an account of Jesus miraculously feeding five thousand people. After this event, the people intended to forcibly make Him their king. Jesus withdrew from them and sought solitude. He was committed to His mission—not the will of the people.
- **Discipline.** Nothing showed Jesus's disciplined life more than his lifestyle of prayer. Matthew 14:23 and Mark 1:35 are just two examples of Him going to secluded places to pray.

In both instances, it was after major ministry moments. He didn't stick around for victory laps after feeding five thousand, and He didn't launch a new ministry or start a podcast after crowds were healed. He modeled discipline and rejected clicks and likes.

- **Humility.** In biblical times, foot washing was an act of hospitality. The act was usually performed by a servant of the host. In the Gospel of John, Jesus turned that tradition on its head by washing the feet of His disciples. Jesus, God in human form, humbled himself as a servant to model his expectations for His followers.

- **Courage.** Going to the cross took courage. Staying on the cross required even more. He had the power at any moment to save Himself as those that mocked Him in Matthew 27 retorted. He kept His absolute authority over all things and heroically died physically, so that He could conquer death and offer us eternal life in Him.

- **Intel, Surveillance, Reconnaissance (ISR).** John 4 is a striking testimony to Jesus's ISR capabilities. His trip through Samaria put the world on notice. He understood the eight-hundred-year feud between the Samaritans and the Israelites. He observed that His followers did not grasp that the Christ came to save the Jew *and* the Gentile. So, his exploration into the land of these people considered traitors was a clear message: He came to seek and save the lost.

- **Action.** Despite the warnings of His followers, Jesus went to Jerusalem *knowing* His murderers awaited. He told His disciples in Matthew 16 that he must go to Jerusalem. Chapter 21 describes His entry. Jesus personified action. He abhorred passivity, pretense, and abdication. He acted in a thoughtful, timely, and thorough manner.

- **Dealing with Failure.** Jesus never failed, but He gave us plenty of examples as to how to deal with failure. Peter denied knowing Jesus in the hours prior to Christ going to the cross. Jesus restored the relationship with Peter and commissioned him to feed people spiritually. In contrast, the failure of the Pharisees was dealt with by Jesus's declaration that the blood of the righteous is upon them (Matthew 23). Jesus showed how to be merciful and how to explain the consequences of disobedience.
- **Delegation.** While Jesus had twelve disciples, he had many other followers. Luke 10 tells the story of His sending out seventy people to cities in advance of His arrival. He didn't simply model this; He wrote the book! He shared the plan, defined success, matched the person to the task, and chose the right work to delegate. Delegation with presence and trust.
- **Flexibility.** The story in John 4, previously referenced in ISR, is an example of Jesus adapting to the needs He encountered as He went. He didn't do what was expected or even most convenient. He flexed His plans for a greater good. He was willing to be interrupted along His mission. His destination was never compromised, but he employed numerous methods to take as many as would follow on the journey.
- **Feedback.** In Mark 9, two of Jesus's disciples, James and John, wanted to call in an aerial strike on some Samaritans who did not receive them properly. They didn't have access to a B-2, so the brothers asked the Lord for permission to call in a strike

from heaven. Jesus rebuked them. His feedback reminded the disciples about their mission of grace and mercy.

- **Evaluation.** In Matthew 17, there is an account of the disciples being unable to heal the son of a man. After healing the boy, Jesus explained to the disciples why their efforts did not result in the desired outcome. Always the teacher, Jesus exposed their lack of faith and understanding. Then, He provided clear instruction for the future.

Phase 3 (Force Multiplier and Expeditionary Guide)

The PhD of leadership is someone who is a force multiplier and an expeditionary guide. A force multiplier is something or someone who can achieve exponentially greater output and effectiveness. The First Special Forces Operational Detachment of the U.S. Army—or Delta—produces these kinds of warriors for the United States. Due to their elite selection process, rigorous training, and ongoing mastery of their skills, a single Delta operator is greater than several other combatants. An expeditionary guide is someone who has experience and success in operating in a vast array of environments while continually advancing toward an objective.

Leaders in this phase understand the following concepts:

- **Strategic and Tactical.** Action, as described in Phase 2, requires the discernment to understand strategic and tactical movement. It would be best to construct a building that is flame resistant in case of a fire, but if a building is on fire, someone needs to run in and save those who are in danger. A leader knows you have to do both. You plan and prepare for the future while being oriented toward action in the present.

- **Joint (*Conducere*).** Joint operations in the military means multiple services are involved such as the Army and the Air Force. Mature leaders destroy silos. Mature leaders understand and enact a philosophy of "Equal Value; Different Responsibilities." The administrative assistant is just as valuable as the supervisor, pastor, or director. Their duties differ; however, duties do not equate to worth. "If you want to go fast, go alone. If you want to go far, go together." Who is the most important person in a long journey? The person reading the map or the person carrying the water? You have to have both. The Latin word *conducere* means "to lead together" or "to bring together." The Conducere Group, led by B.G. Allen, is an outstanding coaching and consulting firm whose goal is to develop teams and individuals that lead together. Aspiring PhDs would be wise to engage the breadth and depth of expertise the Conducere Group offers.
- **Custom Application.** Experienced leaders have a tool belt. They are not one-hit wonders or one-size-fits-all individuals. They customize their approach to the individuals and environment. When someone new joins the staff, an experienced leader understands that change has arrived. The way staff members interact with one another changes. Bonds shift, and alliances move. Leaders recognize in advance that they have to modify their approach to be effective in this new dynamic. Even the leader realizes they have never led this particular group. "Off-the-rack" just doesn't fit. Customizing your approach is required.

- **Closely Examined.** Examination, oversight, and review of a leader never end. When this aspect is overlooked or given only cursory attention, failure can be catastrophic. Even as you read this, your mind can easily recall many stories of unaccountable people of faith who destroyed the lives of others and negatively impacted the church as a whole. A leader, every leader, must have a system placed over them that demands accountability in all Phase 1, 2, and 3 areas. If an individual balks at this idea or tries to manipulate it, their privilege to lead should be immediately revoked. What about grace and mercy? Someone who is unwilling to come under authority or wants to control the manner in which it is exercised, is acting in an ungodly way and should be treated as Jesus treated the Pharisees.
- **Now and Next Generation.** Ralph Nader stated, "The function of leadership is to produce more leaders, not more followers." Additionally, leaders of this quality encourage and celebrate when their apprentices take their own expeditionary steps. I conducted hundreds of interviews for ministerial positions in which the candidate asked me not to contact their current church until late in the screening process, for fear of termination because they were looking for a job. Not only does this smell of dishonesty on the candidate's part, but it reeks of a followership culture at their current church. My disappointment is exceeded only by my anger at this misuse of authority. Leaders should be constantly making investments in other leaders. They should be building the Kingdom—not building their kingdom with fans.

Part Two

John Maxwell says, "Leadership is not an exclusive club reserved for those who were "born with it." The traits comprising the raw materials of leadership can be acquired. Link them up with desire, and nothing can keep you from becoming a leader. Some people have a more intuitive grasp of how to lead than others. These "natural-born leaders" will always emerge, but their influence hinges upon their ability to supplement inborn talent with learned skills. Ultimately, leadership is developed, not discovered."

With the necessary elements of development outlined, how does the church interview and screen people for leadership? I'll conclude this book with my recommendations for a thorough vetting process. There is a wildlife-tour company called the "Fairly Reliable Guide Service." My experience makes me "fairly reliable" in this area, yet we live in a fallen world. Things are missed. The perfect applicant accepts a position, and sin entangles them. In order to mitigate these challenges, the interview, review, and accountability processes never end. Here's a road map.

Background

I worked for Air Force One for two years. When I walked into the interview room, the atmosphere was tense. Seated behind a table were representatives from the Department of the Air Force, the United States Secret Service, and the Special Air Mission, which oversees air transportation for the President, Vice President, First Lady, the presidential cabinet, congressional delegations, and other U.S. and foreign dignitaries. I took my seat and expected an opening salvo such as, "How was your trip?" or "Can we get you some water?" The first inquiry came from a gentleman who cornered the market on a serious face and serious delivery.

"Captain Wiggins, have you ever done anything that, if it became public knowledge, would embarrass the Office of the President of the United States?"

While I'm not Catholic, I've seen plenty of movies where people go to confession. So, I confessed . . . everything. I started with the time I took some baseball cards when I was seven years old from Elmore's, a discount store near our home in East Point, Georgia. I concluded with the speeding ticket I got on the way to the interview (You can't make that kind of stuff up. I got stopped for speeding on the way to my Air Force One interview!). I suppose my criminal background did not rise to the level of dismissal, as I received a call a few days later congratulating me on joining the team.

When I showed up for orientation, I was given a stack of paperwork for a security clearance. I figured this was a mistake. I held a current TS-SCI, meaning Top Secret/Sensitive Compartmented Information. In other words, I already had access to the most-sensitive intelligence information. When I mentioned this to the administrator, he responded that I also needed "Yankee White" clearance. Anyone with direct access to the President of the United States needed further review with a Single Scope Background Investigation (SSBI). This includes in-depth checks of personal and financial history, interviews with a wide range of contacts, and a rigorous evaluation of character and loyalty to ensure trustworthiness for White House-support roles. With no small degree of embarrassment, I returned to my seat and dutifully and willingly completed the forms.

If working for the President required this kind of evaluation, shouldn't an evaluation for having a position of leadership in a church be just as stringent? And, shouldn't the applicant be willing to submit to this type of scrutiny? After a pool of candidates is reduced to a bite-sized number, the remaining applicants should be screened personally, professionally, and financially.

As part of the process, ask the remaining candidates for contacts in all three realms. Don't ask for references. They are worthless. People provide only the names of individuals who will offer glowing reviews. You're not looking for perfection; you're seeking honesty and transparency. Personal contacts should include neighbors who live next door and in close proximity. If the applicant has children, ask for their teachers, athletic coaches, and artistic instructors. Professionally, ask for a complete list of everyone at their current place of employment and proximity of their job to the individual. Next, conduct a financial physical on the applicant and their family. If they ever purchased a car or a house, they provided this information to a loan officer they had never met. Surely, they would be happy to provide this information to fellow spiritual warriors.

In addition to the information above, ask for the names of their three closest friends. If none of these individuals live in close proximity to the person, seek additional names. Physical presence in a person's life matters, otherwise, you know only what the other person wants to tell you. Lastly, ask for a list of names of people the person doesn't like and does not get along with, as well as people who don't like them. Hearing the stories of previous or current conflict is a great preview of coming attractions about future friction.

Interview Teams and Roles

Conduct interviews with a team of at least three, but no more than five. I strongly recommend that one person on the team (Director of Human Resources or similar) attend every interview. This provides for continuity. Prior to the interview, the team should practice. I don't care how many times you've done it—you've never interviewed this person. Ensure that all paperwork that is submitted, including resume, application, questionnaire, and addition assignments, is read by everyone on the team. If someone on the team didn't do their homework, exclude them from the interview. It's the height of arrogance and disrespect to attend an interview without proper preparation. This applies to everyone, regardless of their title. Additionally, the team should sort out the role each member is playing. Who's hosting or facilitating? Is one person taking the lead regarding technical questions, while another person is focusing on character? How will the interview conclude? Also, tell the applicant what the next steps are and when those steps will be completed. Be exact. Saying things like, "We'll be in touch soon" or "We'll call you in a few days" tells me you are either unprofessional or incompetent.

Pitfalls

Watch out for these pitfalls:

- **Order and Priority.** Determine the organization's need prior to considering candidates. It is easy to begin to modify a position into the applicant's strengths rather than holding firm to what the team needs. This can become particularly difficult as a vacancy goes unfilled for an extended period. Just picking *anyone* for a role is more detrimental than having the position open. An unqualified person subtracts from the effectiveness of the entire team.
- **Likeability vs. Compatibility.** Regardless of the personality profile you prefer, each tool recognizes individuals who are "people people." DISC would describe them as "High I" for influence. Myers Briggs has its extroverts, and Big Five has extraversion. People with this tendency can gravitate to liking a person while ignoring if the individual is compatible with the job. Keep in mind that the organization doesn't exist to

hire friends for you. The organization exists to accomplish its mission. Compatibility with the role has to overrule likeability of the candidate.

- **Transfer.** Most churches are averse to conflict and lack accountability. Many label these valuable aspects as "mean" or "un-Christian." An example of this is when an employee underperforms, they are transferred to a different role. Kimberlee Norris, a trial attorney and Co-Founder and Director of Ministry Safe, works with hundreds of churches, non-profits, educational institutions, and para-church organizations around the country. No one sees the culture of more churches than Kimberlee. She cites this *transfer mentality* as an assault on the church. "It tells everyone in the organization, 'If you can't or won't do your job, we will not hold you accountable.' It's deflating for everyone else."

- **Family.** Members of the same family should never be employed by the same church or have parallel volunteer-leadership positions. "But, what about . . . .." *Never.* I've worked in this environment, and it is disastrous. Do you think the wife of a church elder who is working on the staff is going to be disciplined or receive an honest review by their supervisor, knowing their spouse is an overseer? If a child of the lead pastor is employed by the church, it would be foolish to believe that their performance will be evaluated in the same way as everyone else's. Leadership should never allow it. No exceptions. Arguments about how a person is nice, talented, gifted, and the exception to the rule are inconsequential compared to the disruption their hiring causes to the other staff members as well as the church. In case I wasn't clear, *never* employ family members or let them hold significant volunteer-leadership positions.

The Last 10 Percent

- **Work Ethic.** In the interview process, the team must determine a way to analyze the candidate's work ethic. Being a preacher's kid, Kimberlee Norris has seen professional ministry her entire life. This peek behind the curtain allowed her to see areas of compromise. "The church is sometimes willing to accept less than excellence. I see this manifested in marginal work ethic and work effort. You can't instill these qualities, but you can foster, model, and reward them when present." She is also a champion for the Entrepreneurial Operating System (EOS). EOS emphasizes the importance of an individual in a role to "Get it, Want it, Capacity to do it." In the end, you should assimilate only people who have these attributes onto your team.
- **Compensation.** When the applicants have been reduced to a small group, tell them the exact salary and any additional compensation for the position. I see too many churches play "I've got a secret" when it comes to money. Clearly, this doesn't apply to elder, deacon, or other volunteer-leadership positions. It applies for paid staff roles, so, you should be forthcoming with this information. The apostle Paul said a worker is worth his wage. Tell people what you are going to pay them.
- **Feedback.** If an applicant asks for feedback, give it to them. Follow the tenets I described in the chapter on this subject, and be honest. You can be honest and kind simultaneously.
- **Follow-Up.** A member of the interview team should follow up at a pre-determined time that is communicated to the applicant. An electronic method of confirming a time for a telephone call is acceptable, but a telephone call should be made to relay

either "Congratulations" or "Thank you for your interest" to the applicants in the final small group.

There is a leadership vacuum in the church. Many pastors are educated at a seminary. I became acquainted with three seminaries when I started working in a church. These seminaries' attempts at teaching leadership was poorly informed and anemic. Others serving vocationally in the church come from secular-educational backgrounds and join a staff, learning theologically on the job but never developing the skill to lead people toward the very knowledge they acquired. Ministry is not alone in this dilemma. If someone graduates from law school, medical school, or dental school, they have skills to practice their craft but have no understanding of how to lead a law firm, doctor's office, or dental practice. It's absurd to think that, just because someone can draw up a will, treat an ear infection, or extract a tooth, they know how to lead a legal assistant, nurse, or hygienist—let alone an entire business practice. Yet, this analogy plays out in the local church every day. Someone can preach a sermon, connect with students, organize greeters and ushers, and write a Bible-study curriculum, so they believe they inherently understand how to employ leadership principles to invest in a staff and congregation. The folly of this practice leaves me SMH . . . *shaking my head*. It's time to stop admiring and facilitating this problem, and take action. We are in a fight for our spiritual lives. It's time to gird up.

★ ★ ★ ★ ★ ★ ★

Acknowledgments

I'd like to recognize the numerous people who have encouraged me along this journey. "Because I knew you, I have been changed for good."

My family: Leo, Iris, Cathy, Mark, Michael, Robin, Bob, Barbara, David, Charlotte, Susan, Becky, Kenny, Zack, Ben, Scottie, Baker, Shepherd

Bear

Seth and Angela Braker

Elizabeth Busching

Allen Campbell

Colonel Josh Christian

Colonel Tom Coglitore

Beth and Will Dinkins

Kelley Gray

Colonel Denise Hall

Rachel Hobbs

Dr. Russell Levenson, Jr.

Chris and Bo Lindgren

Walter Morris Jr.

MBHS 1980 BS

Joe O'Toole

Patriot Service Dogs

Weyman Prater

Chief Master Sergeant Allen Randall

Julie Sanderson

Victoria Sanderson

Kim Shirley

Grace Munro Warnick

Gloria Webb

Dr. Kelly Wheat

Bob Wolfe

WOOF Program

The men and women I served alongside who allowed me to come home when they didn't

My fellow airmen from 1987 to 2013

- 23rd Tactical Air Support Squadron
- Undergraduate Pilot Training Class 90-15 at Williams AFB, Arizona
- 20th Military Airlift Squadron/15th Airlift Squadron Charleston AFB, South Carolina
- 57th Airlift Squadron, Altus AFB, Oklahoma
- HQ USAF/CVAM, Special Airlift Mission, Pentagon, Washington, DC
- 183rd Airlift Squadron/172nd Operations Group/172nd Airlift Wing, Mississippi Air National Guard
- Officer Training School, Air University, Maxwell AFB, Alabama

★★★★★★★

Glossary of Terms

ACSC—Air Command and Staff College

AFRES—Air Force Reserves

ANG—Air National Guard

AWC—Air War College

BUD/S—Basic Underwater Demolition School

CMSgt—Chief Master Sergeant

CW3—Chief Warrant Officer Three

HF Radio—High Frequency Radio

ISR—Intelligence, Surveillance, Reconnaissance

NSW—Naval Special Warfare

NSWDG—Naval Special Warfare Development Group

OTS—Officer Training School

ROTC—Reserve Officer Training Corps

SERE—Survival, Evasion, Resistance, and Escape

SSBI—Single Scope Background Investigation

SOS—Squadron Officer School

SME—Subject Matter Expert

TS-SCI—Top Secret/Sensitive Compartmented Information

UPT—Undergraduate Pilot Training

USAF—United States Air Force

USAFA—United States Air Force Academy

★★★★★★★

Bibliography

Chapter 1 (Leadership—Is That the Right Word?)

https://geoffaffleck.com/10-best-selling-non-fiction-book-topics/

https://kinginstitute.stanford.edu/king-papers/documents/i-have-dream-address-delivered-march-washington-jobs-and-freedom

Halberstam, David (2002), *War in a Time of Peace: Bush, Clinton, and the Generals,* London: Bloomsbury

Zero Dark Thirty. Directed by Kathryn Bigelow. Columbia Pictures, 2012

Maxwell, John, *Talent Is Never Enough.* Thomas Nelson, Inc.; Abridged edition (January 1, 2007)

Tidying Up with Marie Kondo. Netflix, 2019.

TIME Staff. "The 100 Most Influential People." *TIME,* April 27, 2015.

"100 Greatest One-Hit Wonders." VH1, 2023.

Chapter 2 (Integrity First; Honor Always)

Ryan, John Dale. "Memorandum to All Air Force Personnel on Integrity." Department of the Air Force, 1972.

"Integrity Quotes." AZQuotes. Accessed October 16, 2025. https://www.azquotes.com/

"My Lai Massacre." Wikipedia. Accessed October 16, 2025. https://en.wikipedia.org/wiki/My_Lai_massacre.

Survey conducted from August to September 2025 by Scott Wiggins

Thorsness, Leo. *Surviving Hell: A POW's Journey.* Encounter Books (April 30, 2011)

New American Standard Bible. Grand Rapids, MI: Zondervan, 2002.

https://www.britannica.com/topic/Pashtun

https://en.wikipedia.org/wiki/Pashtuns

Bevere, John. *Honor's Reward: The Essential Reward of Receiving God's Blessing.* FaithWords. November 15, 2007

Chapter 3 (Commitment)

https://www.webmd.com/sleep-disorders/features/10-results-sleep-loss

https://www.goodreads.com/quotes/8713286-age-wrinkles-the-body-quitting-wrinkles-the-soul

https://www.mayoclinic.org/healthy-lifestyle/stress-management/in-depth/positive-thinking/art-20043950

https://ifstudies.org/blog/regular-church-attenders-marry-more-and-divorce-less-than-their-less-devout-peers https://www.britannica.com/science/observational-learning

Virginia Military Institute, Center for Leadership and Ethics. General J. H. Binford Peay III '62 *Leader-in-Residence: Biographies, 2010–2019.* PDF. Accessed October 16, 2025. https://www.vmi.edu/media/content-assets/documents/cle/LIR-bios.pdf.

Cloud, Henry. *Changes That Heal: The Four Shifts That Make Everything Better . . . and that Anyone Can Do*

Lowell Milken Center for Unsung Heroes. "Homepage." October 16, 2025. https://www.lowellmilkencenter.org/

Chapter 4 (Discipline)

Department of the Army. 2020. "Army Regulation 600–20: Army Command Policy." July 24. With administrative revisions dated July 30, 2020; September 1, 2020; February 4, 2021; and July 1, 2021. https://transportation.army.mil/

Department of the Air Force. "Air Force Instruction 36–2903: Dress and Personal Appearance of Air Force Personnel"

Department of the Air Force. 2024. *Air Force Manual 11–2C–17, Volume 3: C–17 Operations Procedures.* August 19. https://static.e-publishing.af.mil/production/1/af_a3/publication/afman11-2c-17v3/afman11-2c-17v3.pdf.

Nieuwhof, Carey. https://careynieuwhof.com/5-things-give-pastors-bad-name-unchurched-people/

New American Standard Bible. Grand Rapids, MI: Zondervan, 2002.

Zelman, Kathleen L. https://www.webmd.com/diet/features/4-steps-healthy-lifestyle#1

Blackaby, Richard and Henry. *Spiritual Leadership*. B&H Books. May 15, 2001.

Lotz, Anne Graham. *The Magnificent Obsession*. Zondervan. August 28, 2010.

Chambers, Oswald. https://utmost.org/classic/discovering-divine-designs-classic/

Ziglar, Zig https://www.brainyquote.com/quotes/zig_ziglar_132507

Chapter 5 (Humility)

Priest, Christopher. *The Prestige*. New York: Touchstone, 1995

Revlin, Russell. *Cognition: Theory and Practice*. Macmillan, 2012.

https://www.airforce.com/education/military-training/ots

https://en.wikipedia.org/wiki/Gerald_Ford

https://www.history.com/news/10-things-you-may-not-know-about-martin-luther-king-jr

Collins, Jim. *Good to Great: Why Some Companies Make the Leap . . . and Others Don't*. New York: HarperCollins, 2001

New American Standard Bible. Grand Rapids, MI: Zondervan, 2002.

United Service Organizations. "USO." October 16, 2025. https://www.uso.org.

Chapter 6 (Courage)

"Online Etymology Dictionary." October 16, 2025. https://www.etymonline.com/word/courage

"Lowell Milken Center for Unsung Heroes." Accessed October 16, 2025. https://www.lowellmilkencenter.org.

"Man Speaks After Rescuing Boy Walking on Hersheypark Monorail." ABC News. Accessed October 17, 2025. https://abcnews.go.com/GMA/Family/man-speaks-after-rescuing-boy-walking-hersheypark-monorail/story/id=125174500.

"Homeless Man Saves Child with Autism from Busy Street." WBAY. August 4, 2025. https://www.wbay.com/2025/08/04/homeless-man-saves-child-with-autism-busy-street/

Buffalo Woman Saves Man's Life Following Vehicle Rollover." WIVB. Accessed October 17, 2025. https://www.wivb.com/news/local-news/erie-county/cheektowaga/buffalo-woman-saves-mans-life-following-vehicle-rollover/.

New American Standard Bible. Grand Rapids, MI: Zondervan, 2002.

https://www.linkedin.com/pulse/bravery-vs-courage-6-types-know-sonia-mcdonald-dickson-

McDonald, Sonia. "First Comes Courage." *Leadership* (November 18, 2020)

Chapter 7 (ISR)

New American Standard Bible. Grand Rapids, MI: Zondervan, 2002.

Berger, Warren. *The Book of Beautiful Questions.* Bloomsbury Publishing. October 30, 2018

Carlin, George. https://www.goodreads.com/quotes/18027-some-people-see-things-that-are-and-ask-why-some

ADP 5-0 (Army Doctrine Publication)

Cordeiro, Wayne. *The Divine Mentor*. Bethany House Publishers. October 1, 2008

Drucker, Peter https://patersoncenter.com/heritage/

Chapter 8 (Action)

Department of the Air Force. *AFMAN 11-2C-17, Volume 1: C-17 Aircrew Training*. [Pentagon]: Department of the Air Force

Goodreads. Accessed October 16, 2025. https://www.goodreads.com/quotes/835515-a-plan-without-action-isn-t-a-plan-it-s-a-speech.

Stanley, Adam. *Next-Generation Leader: Five Essentials for Those Who Will Shape the Future* (Colorado Springs: Multnomah, 2003), 93.

Department of the Air Force. *AFI 11-202, Flying Operations: General Flight Rules. Vol. 3*. [Pentagon]: Department of the Air Force

Batterson, Mark. *Win the Day*. (Colorado Springs: Multnomah, 2020), 83.

New American Standard Bible. Grand Rapids, MI: Zondervan, 2002.

Holiday, Ryan. *Courage Is Calling: Fortune Favors the Brave*. (Penguin Random House, 2021), 92, 102.

Chapter 9 (Dealing with Failure)

Dweck, Carol. *Mindset: The New Psychology of Success*. Ballantine Books. December 26, 2007.

Holiday, Ryan. *The Obstacle Is the Way*. Portfolio. May 1, 2014

Albert Einstein. https://www.goodreads.com/quotes/118182-you-never-fail-until-you-stop-trying

J.K. Rowling. https://news.harvard.edu/gazette/story/2008/06/text-of-j-k-rowling-speech/

Lencioni, Patrick *The Ideal Team Player*. Jossey-Bass. April 25, 2016

New American Standard Bible. Grand Rapids, MI: Zondervan, 2002.

Chapter 10 (Delegation)

www.IMDb.com, *The Bucket List*, 2007, https://www.imdb.com/title/tt0825232/

General Douglas MacArthur, May 12, 1962, Speech at the United States Military Academy

Air Force Doctrine Publication 1-1, Mission Command, August 14, 2023

New American Standard Bible. Grand Rapids, MI: Zondervan, 2002.

Chapter 11 (Flexibility)

Douhet, Giulio. *Command of the Air*, Air University Press, Maxwell Air Force Base, AL, 2019

New American Standard Bible. Grand Rapids, MI: Zondervan, 2002.

Chapter 12 (Feedback)

Department of the Air Force. *AFMAN 11-2C-17, Volume 1: C-17 Aircrew Training*. [Pentagon]: Department of the Air Force

Heen and Stone. *Thanks for the Feedback: The Science and Art of Receiving Feedback Well*. March 31, 2015. Penguin Books.

New American Standard Bible. Grand Rapids, MI: Zondervan, 2002.

Chapter 13 (Evaluation)

Blanchard, Ken. https://www.kenblanchardbooks.com/feedback-is-the-breakfast-of-champions/

Hubbard, Elbert. *John North Willys*. Kessinger Publishing. Reprint September 10, 2010.

Hackman, Richard. https://hbswk.hbs.edu/archive/leading-teams-setting-the-stage-for-great-performances-the-five-keys-to-successful-teams.

Lencioni, Patrick. *The Ideal Team Player*. Jossey-Bass. April 25, 2016

Porter, Michael. https://strategiesforinfluence.com/michael-porter-coaching-tips/

Ephesians 4:11–13. *New American Standard Bible*

New American Standard Bible. Grand Rapids, MI: Zondervan, 2002

The Collected Papers of Roger Harrison. Version 94.10.2. https://bschool.pepperdine.edu/masters-degree/organization-development/content/partone-chapterseven.pdf

Department of the Air Force. *AFMAN 11-2C-17, Volume 1: C-17 Aircrew Training*. Pentagon: Department of the Air Force

Wooden, John. https://www.fitnessmadeclear.com/blog-1/2018/7/23/secrets-of-success-from-the-wizard-of-westwood

Chapter 14 (The Battle Plan)

New American Standard Bible. Grand Rapids, MI: Zondervan, 2002.

"Voltage Control." May 30, 2025. https://voltagecontrol.com/articles/key-leadership-quotes-to-inspire-and-motivate-teams/

Maxwell, John. *How Leaders Develop*. May 3, 2012

★★★★★★★

About the Author

Enjoying a diverse career, Brigadier General Scott Wiggins (U.S. Air Force Retired) has always been a student and practitioner of leadership. He learned through professional stops with the Atlanta Hawks of the National Basketball Association, a twenty-seven-year career as a pilot in the United States Air Force, with noteworthy assignments with Air Force One and the Air Force's Officer Training School, and serving as an executive at one of the largest churches in the country. Today, Brigadier General Wiggins is an executive coach, staff development and leadership consultant. He and his wife, Jennabeth, live in Birmingham, Alabama.

www.ingramcontent.com/pod-product-compliance
Ingram Content Group UK Ltd.
Pitfield, Milton Keynes, MK11 3LW, UK
UKHW021905190726
13853UKWH00002B/519